BUILDING

Lessons Learned in Real Estate and Life

BRIAN WATSON

TABLE OF CONTENTS

INTRODUCTION

"We know what we are, but know not what we may be."

SHAKESPEARE, *HAMLET*, ACT 4, SCENE 5

From the deck of a ship in Ha Long Bay, Vietnam, I become lost in another world. Mist rises off the emerald waters toward the turquoise sky as a moist breeze carries the scent of seawater, fish, and diesel fuel from the dozen barges, junk boats, and kayaks dotting the green horizon. Small, jagged limestone islands and islets tower haphazardly around the mouth of the bay, capped by lush rainforests.

Located in northeast Vietnam, Ha Long literally means "descending dragon," a reference to the local legend that the gods sent fire-breathing creatures to protect native people from invaders and pirates. In turn, the dragons then spit out jewels and jade to form the barrier of islands guarding the open bay. As a UNESCO World Heritage Site, the area's unique geographic features, along with prehistoric evidence indicating the presence of people tens of thousands of years ago, annually attract thousands of visitors eager to explore, hike, rock climb, and scuba dive.

After enjoying Ha Long's ancient beauty as well as other parts of Vietnam, I ventured southwest to Thailand. There, I was immediately struck by the differences between these two similar, yet distinct lands. If one was like going back in time, then the other was like visiting the near future. Equally beautiful with its rolling hills, azure lakes, and stunning coastline, Thailand sharply contrasts with Vietnam in terms of its economic stability, urban advancement, and cultural development. While its culture has grown and prospered tremendously in the last few years, the other has remained mired in place. Where one welcomes visitors from all around the world with ease of entrance, the other requires strict, expensive visas limited to short stays.

One country and culture is certainly not better than the other. Both are captivating, intriguing, and appealing. But Thailand has worked to embrace the future in the midst of preserving its past. Vietnam, on the other hand, reflects timeless beauty but struggles to fulfill its potential as an ambassador of its unique offerings. Simply put, one continues to focus outward, using its resources and opportunities to advance, while the other looks inward, limiting its ability to grow.

This contrast illustrates the essence of what I do as an entrepreneur. As the founder and CEO of a globally focused real estate company, Northstar Commercial Partners, I've learned the importance of honoring historical value as well as embracing a powerful vision for future growth. Both personally and professionally, I've learned that the way a person views the world colors the way they live as well as the way they work. Our attitudes inform our actions. And our attitudes are shaped not only by our circumstances but also by the daily lessons we learn about building a firm foundation while reaching for the stars. Our present ties history to our future.

That's what this book is all about: sharing the lessons I've learned from real estate and real life. While my first book, *The 7 Rings*, focused on balancing life and work with the fulcrum of faith, this book extends those lessons in pursuit of your biggest dreams as well as your greatest gifts to those around you.

Experiencing the differences between countries during my recent visit to Southeast Asia, I realized I had more lessons to share, the kind of experience-based wisdom and hard-won insight that I wish I had known when first starting out. My hope is for this book to be a resource for you, a blueprint as you build your best life, grounded by where you come from and inspired by where you're going. Within these pages, I'll share the best business practices and life lessons gleaned from building a multi-billion dollar global commercial real estate investment firm from nothing.

Forgive me if this sounds immodest, but I know firsthand how being born in the U.S. has enabled me to enjoy a life that others may only dream about. I have been blessed to travel across all regions of our great nation, currently owning assets in 17 states in the U.S. For both work and leisure, I've also visited Central and South America, Africa, Europe, the Middle East, and Asia. While I'm writing from an inherently American perspective, I'm grateful for the many ways my viewpoint has expanded from my global excursions. This book offers my humble way of combining and distilling all of these experiences and sharing them with you.

So many people would do anything to experience the many privileges and freedoms you and I take for granted. Along with millions of others, I'm keenly aware of winning the historical lottery of all time to live when, where, and how we do in this world, especially in the United States of America. Many of us live better than kings and queens of antiquity, given our average life expectancies, access to clean water and healthy food, health and medical benefits, educational options, and our ability to travel around the globe in a matter of hours.

With such abundance comes a responsibility to contribute, to invest, to give back and benefit our planet and fellow human beings in some way.

As with my first book, I do not purport to have all the answers, nor have I led a perfect life. Rather, I have experienced the highs and the lows, from unimaginable achievements to unexpected challenges, that result from living life to the fullest. Because of this real world experience, I offer a uniquely human perspective with the added benefit of lessons learned from some of the world's most innovative leaders, successful entrepreneurs, and wealthiest investors.

Starting with little, I have had the opportunity to build what some consider an empire. This would not be possible without the benefits that freedom, capitalism, and free economic markets have provided throughout my lifetime. My goal is now to equip, empower, and inspire you and others around the world so you can achieve your goals and fulfill your dreams.

We only live once, and each one of us has the opportunity to make a positive or negative difference in this world. My aim is always to make a positive difference, and even if you're the only person who benefits from these lessons I'm about to share, then it's more than worth it. May these lessons ignite your passion to serve your family, your friends, your community—and the world!

Let's roll up our sleeves and start *Building*!

CHAPTER 1

COMING FROM LITTLE, GOING FOR MORE

"People do not decide to become extraordinary. They decide to accomplish extraordinary things."

SIR EDMUND HILLARY

As any builder will tell you, the depth and strength of your foundation determines the size and height of your structure. The firmer your foundation, the higher you can scrape the sky with multiple levels. As a second-generation American, I know firsthand the same is true for bringing your dreams to life. You need structural support to reach for the stars. While I'm indebted to many ancestors for the sacrifices they made, I hold a special place for my grandparents.

My father's parents immigrated to the United States in the early 1900's. My grandfather, Constantine Lambrigger, came from Switzerland and earned a living as a boxer and manual laborer in New York City. My grandmother, Julia Eliasen, arrived from Denmark and worked in a sweatshop as a milliner of hats, a fashion staple for ladies at the time. Both came from humble families in the Old World and risked their futures and everything they knew to build a new and better life for themselves in America.

They first met when my grandfather came to move my grandmother's piano. I'm not sure where she was moving from or moving to or how she even managed to own a piano in the immigrant community in which she lived. Obviously, though, they made some kind of favorable impression on one another. I can just imagine him rolling up his sleeves as beads of sweat poured down his back from the strain of hoisting an upright piano through a window to the ground below. And my grandmother, with all her colorful ladies' hats arranged so neatly along the shelves in her apartment.

On a shelf in my office, a framed black-and-white photograph shows my grandmother standing in front of my grandfather's moving truck at an old gas station with a sign offering "Beer 15¢" in the foreground. I have no idea when it was taken, but it perfectly captures the story of how they met as I imagine it. This picture serves as a daily reminder of my roots and my responsibility to continue fulfilling their American Dream. They sacrificed so much so that their descendants could enjoy a better life filled with opportunities and advantages they never had.

Their hard work led them to further one of their dreams as well. After many years of saving money in the city, they moved to Upstate New York, to the Catskill Mountains. With rugged peaks, open fields, and clear blue lakes, this beautiful area must have reminded them of the homeland they left behind. Which also explains the name for their new venture: The Little Switzerland of America, a small bed-and-breakfast and a cluster of cabins nestled along the shore of the Beaver Kill River, providing modest accommodation to weary travelers.

This river remains quite famous even today as one of the birthplaces of fly-fishing in our country, and nearby the small town of Roscoe is proudly known as "Trout Town U.S.A." I was born not too far away in Middletown and spent the early years of my youth near Roscoe, which I've visited many times since. The fishing is phenomenal, and the beautiful scenery connects me to my family history. When I'm wading in a trout stream beneath a green canopy of trees, I can still hear my grandmother playing the piano that first brought her together with my grandfather, a wistful melody to the rhythm of their dreams.

FAMILY MATTERS

As the first American entrepreneurs on my father's side, my grandparents passed their work ethic and spirit of risk-taking on to my father, Bob Lambrigger, their first son, born in 1938. My father was also the first graduate of the family from high school, and though he never went to college, he started and owned various businesses in construction and real estate, including a campsite, during his life. He taught me many lessons about working hard, about staying positive, about serving your community in love, and about talking to any person about anything. He was a kind, giving, and loving person, and I am so thankful that he was my dad.

Unfortunately, my father passed away in 2016, shortly after my first book, *The 7 Rings*, was published. I remain so grateful that he had the opportunity to read that book, and to see his family name acknowledged and memorialized, as they gave so much to their country, their community, and to me. I'll forever appreciate the unique gifts I received from my dad and from his parents.

I'm also grateful for the special qualities I've inherited from my mother, Carol, and her side of the family. Adopted at birth by the Hanft family in New York—Flatbush in Brooklyn, to be exact—she too had an adventurous spirit and entrepreneurial ambition like my father, whom she married when she was only 17. Following the precedent set by his parents, my father and mother took a risk and acquired Russell Brook Campground in the same area of the Catskills on a sprawling tract of nearly 400 acres. With my father providing the brawn, my mother offered the financial brains of their operation, which included a hunting preserve, horse riding stables, swimming pool, general store, and dozens of campsites.

While sharing a tireless work ethic and entrepreneurial passion, my mother and father remained two different people their entire lives, the proverbial oil and water, and those differences only grew over time. After 21 years of marriage, when I was still quite young, they divorced. Sharing the operation of their dream was ultimately not enough to keep them together. After constantly witnessing their differences and the increased frequency of conflicts, I knew their divorce allowed them each to pursue happier lives apart.

After the divorce, my parents hired a local man named Bill Watson to help run the campsite, and over time my mother and Bill eventually started dating. Soon they decided to move to Colorado and get married, both to start a new life together as well as for the natural beauty of the Western Slope, where we settled as a family.

Bill was an entrepreneur as well, starting and owning a home improvement and construction business, while also running an insurance business. This always-hustle environment shaped my view of the world and my place in it. I was constantly reminded that I came from hard-working stock, from people who came from little but pushed to make a better life—for themselves as well as the generations that followed. Lessons I learned from Mom and Dad, as well as from Bill whom I also came to call my Dad, continue to serve me well, both personally and professionally.

From my mother I learned about tenacity, strength, and being smart about business and investments. Though she did not come from much, she built and owned businesses throughout her lifetime, and supported her family and herself for many years as a single mom. She finally retired at age 75 after working consistently all her life. Today, my mother is more financially stable than most retirees, as she has diligently saved and invested her money for many decades. I'm convinced that she's secretly one of those ladies who keeps money squirreled away in her mattress— literally—as well as in her closet, and beneath the floorboards!

THE WEIGHT OF DUTY

From a very young age, I believed that I was destined to accomplish great things, regardless of my current station in life. I started my first business before I was 12, trying to sell worms. Yes, as a startup it was as unglamorous as it sounds, but it also taught me the basics of supply and demand, profit and loss. During the summers, I also raised and showed livestock for the Montrose County Fair, through 4-H and later Future Farmers of America (FFA).

As someone who came from a family involved in the construction and home improvement business, I learned the value of getting my hands dirty. With my stepfather, Bill, I became a quick study in construction: laying brick, pouring cement, and building with my hands. On the days when I was frustrated or tired of working in the hot sun or frigid winter conditions, Bill would tell me that one day I would be grateful to have a strong work ethic, and to know how to build something with my own hands.

I couldn't appreciate then just how right he was. While I didn't pursue a career swinging a hammer or laying concrete with my own hands, I would nonetheless build a company with my own hands from the ground up. And it's probably no coincidence that my company would help to create countless construction jobs for others willing to work hard and do the best job possible. But at the time, I was like most teens and sometimes resented having to do what felt like such hard labor.

My workload soon became even heavier. When I was 16, Bill passed away suddenly and unexpectedly from an asthma attack. This was very hard on all of us at the time, as Bill was part of the bedrock of our family, and helped to make us a happy, cohesive, family unit. Through his passing, I had to grow up fast and become the man of the house.

When my mother decided to enroll at Mesa State College in Grand Junction an hour away to earn a degree, I had to help take care of my younger sister, Amanda, whom our family had just adopted from Korea, as well as my younger brother, Mark, who was still an infant. While trying to manage at home, I juggled academic responsibilities with student government, sports, Honor Society, and FFA. I also worked at City Market, the local grocery store, sacking groceries for customers and cleaning, while also raising my animals for the county fair each summer.

Most days, the weight of duty pressed in all around me, and there was little time to sit and reflect. Still, I began to feel something stirring deep in my soul. Something to do with who I was and what I wanted to do with my life. A longing for more than I could see in my immediate future. A longing to climb to the top of whatever life had to offer.

GROWING PAINS

Though I loved growing up in small-town rural America, I always felt a bit constrained, just a little too "fenced in." It wasn't the hard physical work and demanding schedule that bothered me as much as wanting the freedom to explore other options and learn new skills. Plus, it always bothered me when someone in my family would whisper, "We're not like those kind of people," referring to the apparent differences they observed in those who appeared wealthy. Curiously enough, their tone almost carried the same kind of judgment others reserved for people who had nothing as the result of laziness or lack of ambition. Somehow we were not supposed to be a part of that larger world that included trips overseas, exotic restaurants, or impromptu purchases. This limiting attitude just didn't sit well with me.

I aspired to learn from and compete with the best, with the highest levels of society, regardless of their position, status, location, or wealth. I never believed that we were "less than" or that we could not achieve whatever we wanted in life. I felt that as being human, we had a right to achieve whatever we wanted, whenever we wanted, as long as we worked hard and smart. I longed to see what it was like in other parts of the world, to watch the sun set behind the Matterhorn or to taste Danish sugar cookies, like the ones my grandmother used to bake, in a café in Copenhagen. People fascinated me—they still do—both our similarities as well as our differences. I longed to learn how business was conducted in other cultures and to understand the important role personal relationships often played in their transactions.

I couldn't have named it at the time, but those growing pains stretched my aspirations beyond the Western Slope. As much as I loved Olathe, the town where I grew up, I sensed that for maximum growth I would have to venture beyond the comfortable familiarity of home. I began to rethink the blueprint for my life that fate had handed me. After Bill's death I was forced to enter adulthood sooner than expected, and that jarring entry also changed my expectations about the future.

I didn't think I was better than anyone else and didn't want to become wealthy as a goal unto itself. I simply wanted to know what I was made of and to test my mettle. Just as my grandparents had left the safety of their homes to venture into an unknown world, I realized it was my turn to do the same. I didn't have to sail across the ocean to Ellis Island like they did, but I did have to travel to an exotic new land—a place called Boulder.

CHAPTER 2

HARDWORK VS. SMARTWORK

*"Far and away the best prize that life
offers is the chance to work hard at
work worth doing."*

--THEODORE ROOSEVELT

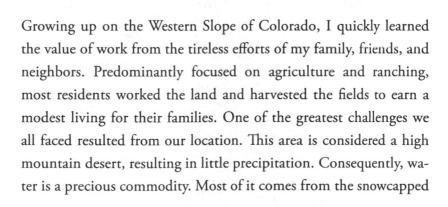

Growing up on the Western Slope of Colorado, I quickly learned the value of work from the tireless efforts of my family, friends, and neighbors. Predominantly focused on agriculture and ranching, most residents worked the land and harvested the fields to earn a modest living for their families. One of the greatest challenges we all faced resulted from our location. This area is considered a high mountain desert, resulting in little precipitation. Consequently, water is a precious commodity. Most of it comes from the snowcapped mountain peaks of the San Juan Mountain Range, with run-offs melting in the summer months to provide water from the previous winter's snowfall.

Crops and pastures for livestock rely on this seasonal water supply for irrigation. From the peaks and foothills of the San Juans, streams rush to the valley floor below and must be channeled by ditches to reach those areas requiring the most water. Each spring, farmers and ranchers had to dig new ditches as well as clear existing ones in order to maximize irrigation on their properties. Our family was no exception, and we had to be ready for these life-giving flows, which came about every two weeks for a couple of days.

I didn't mind digging ditches and working in the often muddy field. Such labor was actually quite fun and even tranquil in its own way, providing routine to both the year as well as those days when the earth's lifeblood nourished alfalfa for livestock, and vegetable gardens. Sweaty and parched at the end of a long day, I felt the satisfaction of seeing the results and knowing that what I did mattered.

But such work was also a bit stressful because we had to be ready for the water, and prepared to be as efficient with it as possible, during these short windows of 48 hours. We often scrambled last-minute to change the flow during the night, move sprinklers with hoses throughout the yard for maximum coverage, and make sure that no drop was wasted. Like most families along the Western Slope, we literally had to plan our vacations or trips away from the house, based on the water schedule. Friends and neighbors would be consumed with their own water work so we couldn't ask anyone to irrigate for us. We had to be there or risk missing this precious resource. Most people, even in a dry state like Colorado, often overlook the priceless necessity of water to give life to arid soil.

BRAIN OVER BRAWN

From digging water irrigation ditches, I learned one of my life's greatest lessons: the difference between what I call "hardwork" and "smartwork." Hardwork is the kind of backbreaking labor required to take shovel in hand and carve straight ditches in arid, rocky soil. Such effort produces many blisters and callouses on your hands along with a sore back. Dry heat and fierce winds leave your face and arms feeling like they've been sandpapered. Even with sunglasses, you still get blowing grit and swirling dust in your eyes. Hardwork is honest, valuable labor invested in physical effort and skillful determination to complete a job that has to be done. But it's not necessarily the best, most efficient way to get some jobs done.

Smartwork, on the other hand, supplements muscle power with brainpower. It multiplies energy invested in a task by using intelligence, experience, and instinct for maximum results. This mindset develops a strategy that allows you to use your gifts, talents, and resources to accomplish the most results for the least amount of time. Smartwork always asks, "What is the highest and best use of my *personal* time?" rather than assuming your time is of equal value as anyone else's.

Applied to water irrigation, smartwork inspires you to consider whether to use a tractor or plow for your ditches or to invest money up front in plastic pipes that will ultimately retain and deliver more water than allowing it to be lost in dirt ditches that often need to be re-dug or cleaned out from plant growth. Depending on your other skills and work opportunities, it might be smarter to hire someone else to manually dig ditches while you focus your energy and attention on more lucrative endeavors.

We all have specific talents, experiences, and capabilities. No one person can or should be expected to excel in every area or to master every skill. We are each unique with certain natural abilities, life experiences, and personal perspectives that should influence how we think about the work we do. Given your particular life experiences and outlook, how best are you suited to use your time and energy wisely?

We each have finite resources—our time, our talent, and our treasure—to invest in a limited number of accomplishments in this life. Knowing our hours, expertise, and finances are limited, we have to consider how best to leverage them in order to achieve our goals and fulfill our individual dreams. If you hope to be productive and successful in life, then you must regularly ask yourself: *How should I use my unique resources to maximize my personal impact and produce the greatest results?*

PRESS THE EASY BUTTON

Our time on this earth is limited. No matter how successful, talented, wealthy, or ambitious, we each only get 24 hours each day. We must decide daily what should get our energy, attention, and best efforts. If your day is consumed by tasks that just drain time, or that are not conducive to your highest goals and the best use of your talents, then something must change if you desire to make the most of your life. Identify these time-drainers, both large and small, and consider eliminating, streamlining, or allocating them to others. You would be surprised how many "urgent" or "important" tasks can be shifted if you step back and look at them from a larger perspective.

For example, my father owned a residential real estate company in the small town of Roscoe in Upstate New York. The summer after I graduated from college, I worked for him brokering the sale of residential properties. During that summer I quickly observed the way my dad believed that he had to do every aspect of the business himself in order to make sure it was done to his satisfaction. As an example, he would drive throughout the extensive area he served checking on the real estate marketing signs placed in front of properties, trimming the grass or repositioning them for better visibility. He thought this ongoing maintenance was a good use of his time instead of having the homeowner keep these areas clean on their lawns or hiring a teenager to drive around and do it for minimum wage.

Clearly, the highest and best use of my father's time, at least from my vantage point, would have been to run the real estate office, manage his other sales agents, and build relationships to secure new listings. The commissions from one new listing and subsequent sale alone could probably have paid for a helper for many years to come, versus having my father spend his time and energy pulling weeds and trimming grass. Beyond the economic impact, delegating this responsibility would have reduced my father's stress load and given him more quality time to enjoy with his family rather than having to run around doing everything himself and never having a moment's rest.

I remembered what I had witnessed with my dad many years later at a Toastmasters meeting. As a young professional working in commercial real estate in downtown Denver, Colorado, I wanted to become a better communicator and public speaker. At one of our meetings, I heard another person give a speech about "pressing the easy button," playing off of a marketing campaign popular at the time from the retailer Staples. Although it was a simple, three-minute speech, the message resonated that day and stayed with me.

The speaker basically outlined that we should each "press the easy button" in life by allocating our time wisely and efficiently. For instance, if you have your clothes dry cleaned, should you drop off and pick up the cleaned clothes yourself, or "press the easy button" and have the dry cleaning company drop them off at your workplace or residence? The latter frees you up with more time that you can then allocate to more productive aspects of your life. Given the number of online services and phone apps, we can find a service to do just about any of the routine maintenance tasks on our to-do list from walking our pets to grocery shopping. There are even trainers with portable gyms that will come to your home or workplace in order to make it easier to work out.

What should you be doing to "press the easy button" and allocate your time and talents wisely?

THE BIG THREE

When I founded my company decades ago, I had to do all aspects of the business: handling calls, scheduling appointments, handwriting checks for bill payment, identifying properties, researching titles, closing deals, and many other tasks. As the company grew, I was able to hire others for tasks that were not the best use of my personal time, allowing me to create greater value and opportunity for the firm. Now my company has grown and employs more people than I ever imagined—which means I have to delegate and stay focused on the big picture of how we continue to succeed.

Regularly, I evaluate what I'm doing that I shouldn't be doing, and who should I either move within the company to address these areas, or I should hire to handle specialized areas. As part of this process, I focus on hiring people who can do a better job than I would do in that task. I have no problem hiring team members who are smarter, more experienced, or naturally talented in their area of specialty. Though they are experts in their specific roles, I'm the captain who sees where we're going, sets our course, and adjusts our sails based on current conditions. Over the years I've learned to focus on three big areas where I can add the most value at my firm: setting the strategy, hiring the best team members, and cultivating key relationships. Let's consider each of these in a little more detail.

SETTING THE STRATEGY

As the founder of the company, I'm the only person with the institutional knowledge of where we started and all of the developments since then. I also helped to assemble the team and intimately understand our execution capabilities given our history and current personnel. Part of my role requires meeting and learning from investors, vendors, lenders, tenants, and strategic leaders throughout the U.S. and the world. All of these conversations and learning opportunities help me to formulate our investment strategy and its execution, as I get to see the cumulative perspective of these various stakeholders. The ability to see through the layers is not easy but necessary in order to anticipate changes in the market. My comprehensive vantage point affords me a unique perspective for setting the investment strategy and implementing its activation.

HIRING THE BEST TEAM MEMBERS

As a public school kid who rode the bus to and from school, I learned that different passengers created different dynamics on those rides to and from school. Similarly, hiring the right people for the right seats on your "company bus" is essential if we're going to move forward in the right direction. This one may sound easy, but it is one of the most challenging aspects to building any successful company. As you populate your bus, you have to decide what people you want riding with you and whether they're capable and willing to travel at the required speed to reach your destinations. Depending on where you want to go, and what you want to achieve, you may want different people to go with you. You also have to make sure that they are sitting in the right seats and that they're willing to contribute and work as part of a team. When I started the company, it was just me as the driver of the bus and an assistant. Over the years, we have been fortunate to invite different people along for the ride while others left when we reached their stop.

CULTIVATING RELATIONSHIPS

The dynamics of people working together change constantly and require ongoing cultivation. Whether with employees, clients, vendors, or other stakeholders, your relationships determine the future of your company. Connecting with investors and growing strategic relationships for the company requires time, effort, and a certain willingness to be known. Not everyone has the desire or ability to meet and connect with diverse people from around the world. Relational chemistry is a unique gift and can't be faked or contrived, although it can be cultivated and developed over time. I'm fortunate in that I naturally love to connect with people. As I develop relationships that offer larger impact for the company, I encourage my team to extend our network by following through on business we bring in. This allows the team to "rack and stack," while I grow quality meaningful relationships that create a larger deal flow for us.

ONLY DO WHAT ONLY YOU CAN DO

If I contribute my best to these three endeavors, while empowering my team to do the same, then we will achieve better and better results together each year. By meeting regularly, communicating openly, listening attentively, and implementing ideas quickly, we will reach new heights.

This is in stark contrast to assuming that I have to do everything in the firm, or that no one can do everything as well as I can. As a team, we can divide and conquer more together while also enjoying life-work balance and relationships with family and friends. In fact, I learned this lesson from a friend of mine, who owns a similar company. Though he has been very successful financially, he has paid a dear price for it in his numerous marriages, frequent staff turnover, and stress-related health issues.

You see, this person feels that he is the only person who can do things as well as he does, and that his people are incompetent. Consequently, he doesn't empower his people to achieve, and as they work under a culture of fear, they will not make decisions, which only creates more work for him. Though he has much from a financial perspective, he has little from a quality of life and personal time perspective.

The most effective people in life master the art of defining what their most impactful contributions can be and learn to empower others to handle the other tasks. Focus on the projects, tasks, and big-impact actions that only you can do—leave the rest to others. Determine what you do best and what contributions will help "move the needle" the most in the direction you want to go. Shed the other time-consuming tasks and empower others to do them. When you focus your energies on what only you can do, you will be a more productive, more effective, and happier person.

Work hard but always work smart!

CHAPTER 3

THE POWER OF DIVERSITY

"We should all know that diversity makes for a rich tapestry, and we must understand that all the threads of the tapestry are equal in value no matter what their color."

--MAYA ANGELOU

After graduating from Olathe High School on the Western Slope of Colorado in 1989, I decided to attend the University of Colorado at Boulder. While CU Boulder is a great school, at the time my choice reflected the reality that I had to pay for my own college education. My stepfather, Bill, had passed away the previous year, and my mother, with two pre-school-aged kids at home, was not in a financial position to help me. Just a few months before Bill's passing, they had adopted my sister, Amanda, from Korea, and then welcomed my brother, Mark, an unexpected blessing since my mom was then 42 years of age.

As an in-state school, CU Boulder was more affordable than out-of-state colleges, and they also gave me some scholarships and financial aid, including being a part of the President's Leadership Class, a program that targeted young leaders and provided further training. By receiving scholarships, shoveling horse stalls, landscaping part-time, and entering the work-study program for students from lower income families, I was able to pay my way through college. The sacrifices and hard work were often challenging, but there was never any doubt about my commitment to achieve a college education.

TASTE THE DIFFERENCE

Growing up in the small town of Olathe, I rarely encountered anyone who was very different than my family and friends. In comparison to large cities and urban areas, there was simply little diversity of any kind, whether economic, cultural, or racial. Boulder, thanks in part to the large, diverse student body of CU, opened my eyes to people from a variety of cultures, religions, and ethnic backgrounds. In addition to welcoming diversity of thought, the presence of the state's eponymous university attracted individuals and industries from around the world.

As a small town kid from an agricultural and ranching community, I loved the vibrant differences thriving on campus. Meeting so many new people who, at first glance, appeared so different, I quickly developed a deep appreciation for the variety of ideas, practices, languages, experiences, and cultural influences swirling around me. I also enjoyed trying new ethnic foods at the numerous restaurants around Boulder.

Soon after arriving, I discovered Ras Kassa's Ethiopian Restaurant, an immediate favorite that I still frequent to this day. Owned by a woman from Ethiopia, this restaurant provided an authentic cultural experience, featuring small stools instead of chairs, sharing meals together communally—or what we called "family style" back in Olathe, and using only your hands instead of utensils. Savoring the delicious lamb stew and homemade injera bread there, I felt like I was in another world!

A SEMESTER AT SEA

Although I had never traveled outside the U.S. while growing up, mainly due to the cost, I suspect, my attraction to other world cultures led me to a life-changing experience: joining the Semester at Sea program during my junior year at college. Strolling across campus, I often saw placards advertising this unique educational experience, and it intrigued me.

Semester at Sea operated a cruise ship equipped with classrooms, which sailed around the world with a few hundred college students, professors, and sailors each semester. Students could take college classes on board and receive credit for these back at their respective universities. As someone of modest means, I first assumed I couldn't afforded this program but then applied for its work-study program, which basically meant serving the other students who didn't require such financial aid.

I had already shoveled horse stalls when I first arrived in Boulder and was then working in the business school's library as a work-study student to cover my tuition so I was happy to work my way around the world, enjoying this priceless educational voyage. As it turned out, my job onboard suited me: I was to create and publish our ship's daily newspaper, which forced me to keep up with news on board the ship as we travelled. I not only would be meeting hundreds of people from throughout the U.S., but I would also become a student of current events in our travels.

In the spring of 1992, we sailed from the Bahamas to Venezuela, then on to Brazil, from there to South Africa, to Kenya, to India, to Malaysia, to Taiwan, to Hong Kong, and finally to Seattle, Washington. We spent a few days in each port and were allowed to explore as we wished, to conduct research and apply lessons from our classes, and generally just to explore new cultural experiences. Some students clearly came from tremendous wealth, usually checking in to luxury hotels in our various ports of call before sending the spoils of their shopping sprees back to family and friends in the States.

TRAVELING LIGHT

I, on the other hand, became an expert at traveling light. Either I'd make day trips with my backpack slung over my shoulder and return on board the ship each night, or I'd find cheap lodging while roaming through small towns and along the countryside. When we docked in Venezuela, for example, I went into the barrio and joined a pick-up basketball game with some kids, one of whom invited me to join his family for a simple meal of beans and rice that evening. Later, after most of the family had gone to bed, I sat up listening to old men talking in a language I didn't know, while they drank and smoked and laughed. My body ached from exerting myself in the basketball game, but I knew I'd never forget the scent of tobacco smoke on the humid air or the soft, staccato music of their voices floating into the night sky.

Semester at Sea was a defining experience for me. Traveling around the world and absorbing all the people, places, images, and events transformed a small-town hayseed with limited exposure into a man who cherished the value of diverse cultures, exotic foods, unique backgrounds, and surprising customs. Instead of seeing the sites of one or two countries while on vacation for a couple weeks, I sailed into new countries for several months. Semester at Sea placed me in an environment of requiring constant change, daily flexibility, and personal adaptability.

For many years, I believed my time sailing around the world while in college put a travel bug in my soul. But as I continued to travel to new ports and meet our world's diverse peoples, I realized that Semester at Sea only revealed a part of myself that was there all along: a passionate curiosity waiting to explore and soak-in the joys that come from tasting cardamom coffee in Morocco or watching native dancers synchronized in neon-colored costumes in Malaysia. Simply put, I love to explore, learn from, and build relationships with diverse people from throughout the world. This appreciation and understanding of diversity has given me a unique perspective, as I have learned to love people of all backgrounds.

As human beings, we're more alike than different. But each culture has something to offer, which in turn makes us wiser, more capable, more empathetic, as we get to know them and appreciate them. We're so much richer for being open to knowing more about the different cultures and communities of people who inhabit the earth with us. Thanks to social media, now more than ever, we're neighbors, no matter how much distance may seem to be between us.

DEAL OR NO DEAL

The way I negotiate complex business deals today began over two decades ago on the streets of Caracas and Hong Kong, haggling over the price of an item I hoped to buy. My skills were later tempered with patience from working throughout the Middle East and Japan, and made more acute by bartering in India. The art of getting a good deal, not being taken advantage of, being able to walk away and have the price quickly reduced by the vendor as they call you back to the negotiation, all while being respectful, is priceless.

In the West, we aren't used to bargaining when we buy something. Even when we pursue negotiating a purchase instead of paying the asking price, we cling to the notion of "meeting in the middle," which others from different cultures strategically use against us by continuing to haggle. Our mindset of not wanting to offend someone different than we are and our expectation of having to see a price tag on items often gets in our way of getting the best deal. Negotiating a purchase, whether great or small, whether in a small market in Rome or a boardroom in Moscow, requires insight into the cultures represented in the exchange. If we're not shrewd about understanding the rules of the game, then we automatically allow others to get better terms as we pay them a higher price than necessary. Often, it's not guilt about the economic price paid, but the complete list of give-and-take terms required.

Interacting with diverse people from around the world always makes you a stronger negotiator and dealmaker. Whether you're a CEO bidding on a contract with a foreign corporation or a tourist on holiday buying a unique souvenir, it helps to understand cultural differences and human psychology. It's not only acceptable to negotiate in virtually every world culture, it's actually expected and can be quite fun. Some sellers might even be offended if you're not willing to play the game. The vendor knows you want their product or service, and you know they may want your dollars, but you are only willing to give so much before seeking out their competitor who may gladly accept your terms. All the while you must keep in mind that you may not find another vendor with that product or service that you want, so you must work the art of the deal flexibly but firmly.

TEAM DIVERSITY

Another aspect of diversity that I appreciate is the way it expands perspectives within a collective group. Teams, whether on the football field or in the conference room, are stronger when individual members bring uniquely different viewpoints. Being able to see from multiple cultural, social, and sociological angles eliminates blind spots and often provides surprising solutions. There is not only strength in numbers but in diversity of thought.

If we all look, act, and think the same, we're more vulnerable to loss. We won't be able to recognize the opportunities as well as potential threats coming our way. When you assemble a team that's distinctly diverse, then the group dynamic allows for dialogues, discussions, and innovations that a homogenous group might never produce.

When a variety of individuals come together, each with a different background and perspective, then the ability to spark a new idea, company, or capability only increases. I'm convinced that America's diversity is one of our greatest assets and one of the main reasons we've been so successful in our growth and development since its founding.

Unlike some cultures that remain homogenous or believe that "outsiders" can't add value, the United States has long been recognized as a great melting pot of individual cultures blending together to form a flavorful new dish. Historically, our country has encouraged diversity of thought and action. This in turn, has made us more productive, and has taken some of the best attributes of many cultures to form the uniqueness of our shared American experience. Diversity makes us stronger, better, more interesting, more enjoyable, and more capable. I would never want to live in a world where we all talk, act, think, and look alike. Such a place would quickly become boring and bland, lacking the spicy friction resulting from the interaction of different people.

Whenever I speak or lead group discussions for entrepreneurs and community leaders, I stress the vital importance of including all people and celebrating our differences together. Whether you're developing your team at work or enriching your own personal life, seek out people and ideas that are different from your own, that challenge you, that make you ask more questions and develop new ideas, that make you feel uncomfortable at times. You might be surprised how much more fulfilling your life can be when you're willing to receive what others are so generously willing to share with you.

Recently I interviewed and then hired a new person for my firm. After the initial interview and tour of my office, he gave me one of the best compliments that I've received by stating that my company was the most diverse commercial real estate firm he had ever seen in terms of age, gender, race, and diverse backgrounds. This is one of the reasons that Northstar Commercial Partners has been so successful.

BUILDING TRUST

We're all well aware that we're now involved in a global economy, and that the world is only getting smaller. We each must grow and adapt to this, as individuals as well as leaders and business owners, or we will lose out on economic and experiential opportunities. Being comfortable, accepting, and fluent with diverse people is now the global currency of success.

As my company has grown during the past two decades, I have had the opportunity to combine my love of travel with my pursuit of new business. Though the vast majority of equity investors in our commercial real estate investments come from the United States, I've made a diligent effort to expand these capital relationships to other countries as well. My goal remains to diversify and broaden our investor base, especially since a tremendous amount of foreign capital investors would like to participate in U.S. economic opportunities. In addition, I enjoy meeting, learning from, and building quality relationships with these individuals from the global community.

My business has taken me to Europe, the Middle East, and Asia. At times, I visit one country per day, traveling to places like Dubai, from there to Oman, then to Bahrain, to Saudi Arabia, to Lebanon, and then home all in one week. These capital-raising excursions allow me to break bread with investors in Israel, or stay with an investor and his family in Shanghai, or sip fine teas and ales in London with professionals from various investment houses, family offices, and financial institutions.

On some occasions, I wake up in a hotel room and have to remind myself which country I'm in. After so much travel and so many hotels, I always take a photo of my hotel room number so I know where to return at the end of the day. Nonetheless, such travel is invigorating and exciting, to the point where it's sometimes hard to sleep more than a few hours per night. Recalibrating to new time zones, I often start when my friends, family, and staff in the States are going to bed. After strong coffee and a bite to eat, I attend meetings throughout the day, follow my colleagues' cue for lunch, and often finish with a late business dinner.

Many cultures don't eat their evening meal until as late as 9 or 10 p.m. so by the time I return to my hotel room, it might be near midnight. With U.S. time zones often 6-12 hours behind my current one, many times I then get wrapped up in phone calls and emails. I've often said that I do two jobs at once while traveling overseas: the work on the ground building investor relationships and the usual work back at home. After doing emails and taking conference calls from midnight to 3 a.m., I fall asleep and prepare to repeat the sequence all over again the following day.

But I wouldn't trade it for anything. Working with international investors has given me a better appreciation of other cultures and has given me the opportunity to meet new friends and their families. Northstar remains an entrepreneurial company, and this attitude of taking calculated risks and exploring new possibilities continues to help us grow. As I've expanded my relationships beyond the boardroom, I've learned about my investors and their cultures on a personal level. No matter how different or similar we may be, the most important exchange made involves understanding and trust.

Trust is vital before business can be done. This can often frustrate some people who want to finish small talk only as a prerequisite for getting down to business and closing the deal. But this attitude overlooks the personalities, families, cultures, and countries involved. You can never strip the humanity from a negotiation. Therefore, it's always best to build relationships before you build a skyscraper.

In many cultures, the small talk is sometimes the most important part of the deal, as they want to get to know you. This interaction includes a constant weaving in and out of business discussions, sipping coffee, eating locally sourced food, discussing family, and a host of other nuanced topics that must be respected and properly developed.

Once you build this understanding and trust together, you have partners for life.

These partnerships, like all relationships, require ongoing investments of time, attention, and shared experiences. Sometimes it takes many visits over several years before someone is willing to commit to a deal together. At other times, some multi-million dollar projects come together in a matter of minutes based on the first impression others have. Either way, it's a process, an ongoing relationship that enables me to grow. I get to see the world on a deeper level, build quality friendships, and enjoy amazing experiences.

Embrace, celebrate, and seek out diversity, for it is one of the great gifts of this world.

CHAPTER 4

HUNT AND KILL— COMPETITION AND COMMISSION

"Sales are contingent upon the attitude of the salesman—not the attitude of the prospect."

--W. CLEMENT STONE

After graduating from CU Boulder in May of 1993, I went to work at my father's residential real estate office in Upstate New York. This was located in the very small town of Roscoe, New York, famous for the Beaver Kill River and its rich history of fly-fishing. Most of my father's customers were from New York City and wanted a second home or weekend getaway, somewhere they could escape the frenetic pace and stress of urban living and enjoy natural beauty and peaceful surroundings. Compared to the exorbitant prices of city living, homes in the area were not very expensive, making them affordable for a variety of individuals and families looking for a relaxing retreat from apartment living and the asphalt jungle.

While making plans to join the Peace Corps, I agreed to work for my dad as a residential sales broker, marketing properties he represented and targeting these second-home buyers. This would be my first job paid entirely on commission. I will always remember the first home I sold, a modest little residence, to a couple from New York City. Each time they came up to look at potential properties, they brought along their son, who had Down Syndrome. They had saved up money for many years in hopes of buying a home in the countryside, a tranquil place that he would especially enjoy. The noisy, crowded clamor of the city often compounded their son's stress, and they wanted him to experience a more peaceful environment free of rushing commuters and honking taxis. The little house they bought, off a quiet country road, had green shutters and a nice yard, at least by city standards, and promised to be a haven for them and their son.

PASSION PLUS PERSEVERANCE

By the end of the summer 1993, I had earned almost $15,000, which was a tremendous amount of money at the time, especially for a 21 year old. For only three months' work, I had earned what some other real estate agents in that area pulled in for their entire year. This financial cushion came in handy when, much to my disappointment, my Peace Corps opportunity fell through due to an allergy I had as young child. Missing the mountains of the West, I decided to move back to Colorado, where I hoped my training from that summer would provide me with some lessons to work with a commercial real estate brokerage firm.

One of the top companies in Colorado at that time was Cushman and Wakefield (C&W), an international concern headquartered in New York. I soon discovered, however, that they were not hiring new brokers at the time. Like most large corporate firms, they were only interested in hiring a "seasoned sales professional"—in other words, someone with more than a few residential sales over a summer in Upstate New York. While I managed to get my foot in the door for a preliminary conversation at Cushman and Wakefield along with a few of its competitors, I quickly realized they had little interest in letting an ambitious young adult prove himself.

After looking at other options, none of which interested me as much as C&W, I became more determined (others might say desperate!) to find a way into my first choice, Cushman and Wakefield. So I called them about every other day for several weeks, insisting that I could add tremendous value to their firm if they would only give me a chance. While their area managing director and senior brokers continued to take my calls, they were unwilling to offer any possibility of a position. Realizing I wasn't getting anywhere fast, I finally made them an offer they couldn't refuse: *I would work without pay.* After I had demonstrated my abilities, if they liked what they saw, then we could discuss a paid position. But in the meantime I just wanted to work for them.

My gamble paid off. They were either impressed by my confidence and perseverance or had enough pity on my dogged persistence to put me out of my misery. They agreed and I started my self-created volunteer position the following week. You can just imagine how I pulled out all the stops to impress them and show my determination, dedication, and drive. I must have proved myself because they indeed liked what they saw and agreed to hire me. Later, after working there for sometime, I realized that my passion, tenacity, teachability, and bold risk-taking are traits that usually define a successful broker.

In my experience, passion plus perseverance is ultimately unbeatable.

SPACE FOR SUCCESS

The training program at Cushman and Wakefield was largely hands-on and experience-based. It included working for some senior brokers, flipping through the contact books, making phone calls, and cold-calling tenants of desirable properties. Many days, I would start at the top floor of a building and literally knock on each door, handing each tenant a flyer for space availability in another building and trying to secure the business card of their office's decision maker. After covering all floors, I would then move on to another building. Once I had blanketed at least three or four, I would categorize these buildings, call upon the decision maker by phone, and hope to either secure their tenancy at the other property I was marketing or secure a tenant representation assignment to help them search for new space and negotiate an acceptable deal at another property.

The work rewarded consistency, making a lot of cold calls, follow through, determination in the face of "no," and attention to detail—a nice way of saying it was often tedious, frustrating, and disappointing. With so many hours invested, I only got paid my commission in halves—the first when a new lease agreement was signed and the rest when the tenant took occupancy, which was often several months later or even a year after the space had been built-out or remodeled to suit their specific needs.

Nonetheless, I found the challenge exciting. Each new door that I knocked on or phone call that I made could lead to something great. At the end of the day, it was a numbers game based on the law of averages. The more doors knocked on and calls made, the greater the chance of securing a deal and getting a payday, which might consist of a few thousand dollars or a few million. This was a business of no floors and no ceilings for potential income, which I thrived in and still do to this day. I am not the type of person who would be happy with the same paycheck amount every other week as my compensation.

Although my circumstances are wildly improved, I still have this same mindset today. Instead of resting on past successes or waiting on opportunities to present themselves, I consider each day full of countless possibilities. Although I'm knocking on different doors and calling people who are happy to hear from me, I invest my energy in creating the space for success—both literally and figuratively. In order to be successful, you must take action instead of hoping and waiting for business to come to you.

THRILL OF THE HUNT

Like most traditional brokerage environments, Cushman and Wakefield associates were paid entirely by commissions. As harsh as it may sound, the basic dynamics were simple: If you wanted to eat, then you had to go hunt and kill. Though you could set your own hours and pursue your own strategy, if you didn't work hard and smart, your production would suffer and you wouldn't earn enough to live on. The notion of setting your own hours or working at your own speed was a fallacy. If you wanted to be productive and successful, then you worked as hard as possible all the time. If you didn't bring in enough income for the firm and yourself, then you were fired.

With no ceiling cap on income, and no base salary as a safety net, I was motivated, like so many other commission-based salespeople, to make work a part of everyday life. This was honestly nothing new but just an extension of the work ethic that had been ingrained in me while growing up. Working as a broker of commercial real estate suited me then because I wasn't really working for the company as much as working for myself. I was not only striving to survive but to get ahead and further my dreams.

I grew to love this commissioned based environment and appreciated the way I was rewarded for my creativity, effort, and execution. I could concentrate on one big deal or work a dozen at once and be compensated for the ones that closed. This approach taught me to develop a multi-task mindset and always keep multiple irons in the fire, knowing that all deals won't close—at least not when you hope or expect. You need to develop back-up strategies and keep potential opportunities growing. I learned to juggle and cultivate relationships, new properties, and potential deals all at different stages of the process.

Some deals would close fast, others could take years, and some would die out due to the requirements going away. I learned to make progress, whether a little or a lot, each day on each different deal. Some days one deal might move forward an inch while another was crossing the finish line. On tough days, I would lose ground, knowing the time was clicking away on the clock. The goal was always to stay in the race and push multiple transactions to completion.

Though being 100% commission-based is not for everyone, I recommend trying and learning from it, especially if you want to be in the real estate business. Working on commission teaches you so many valuable lessons about the industry, including the importance of the momentum of a deal, the ability to negotiate and understand value drivers and enhancements, and the various roles of stakeholders in the industry. It's an exhilarating profession, especially when your hard work pays off and all the pieces come together.

RAIN OR SHINE

There's another, often unseen, value to being commission-based: it teaches you how to handle your money and live within your budget. With commissions, you may close a large deal or several deals that generate a significant amount of income. There will also be times of income drought. If you spend all of your money in the good times expecting that the income will always be there at the same level, it's painful when deals fall through and you're left without commissions.

This financial ebb and flow reminds me of the monsoon season in Africa. When the heavy rains come, the vegetation grows lush and members of the animal kingdom have plenty of water and food. The animals flourish, gain weight, reproduce, and easily complete their life cycles. When the rains stop, however, water can dry up fast, and food becomes scarce. Animals become agitated and go hungry and in extreme cases starve, making them vulnerable to other predators and the environment, sometimes costing their very lives.

Similarly with commissions, sometimes there's plenty and you have much, and sometimes it goes lean and you do without. Accept the reality of this up-and-down cycle and be wise about budgeting, saving, and spending your financial resources. While we can't control the rainfall in nature, we can control how we save and utilize our financial reserves in living a commission-based lifestyle. Learn the rhythm of your spending and adjust it to the pace of your earning, all while saving enough so the beat goes on.

SIMPLY THE BEST

Commercial real estate is highly competitive. Becoming a successful, commercial real estate broker is not for the faint of heart or the thin-skinned person. Because there's the potential for large paydays and huge commissions, the industry attracts a variety of aggressive, highly motivated, and talented individuals who enjoy the intense competition. Most have college educations, international training, and hard-won experience.

These brokers are the best of the best, and instead of being intimidated or threatened by their success, you discover many of them inspire you to new heights and challenge you to be the best that you can be. Unfortunately, some of them can also be unethical, conniving, and ruthless so you always need to stay sharp and keep focus. If you enjoy competition at the highest levels, then there's no better playing field for you. On the other hand, if you prefer a steady, consistent paycheck and ongoing security, this field may prove too stressful for you.

I'm a firm believer that competition makes everyone and everything better—products, services, teams, corporations, and individuals. Competition acts as a refining fire for each us, and the higher the temperature and pressure, the sooner we can be transformed from lumpy pieces of coal to brilliant diamonds. Forgive me if it sounds cliché, but it's true!

If you can take the pressure, value the competition, and rise to the occasion, then you will be a better, more capable person. Honing your best against the best of others will only make you stronger, smarter, and sharper in pursuit of fulfilling your dreams. Competition ultimately forces you to compete with yourself, revealing new depths of drive and determination. If you're willing to compete in life, to always do better than you did the day before, then regardless of whether you get the next deal, you will always be a winner!

CHAPTER 5

ENJOY THE RIDE 20 LESSONS FROM AN ENTREPRENEUR

"If we did all that we are capable of doing, we would literally astonish ourselves."

--THOMAS EDISON

In the year 2000, I founded Northstar Commercial Partners, in a few hundred square foot office above the current Ted's Montana Grill on Larimer Square in downtown Denver, Colorado. After working as a commercial real estate broker for Cushman & Wakefield in Denver for the prior seven years, I decided it was time to test my wings and fly on my own. As determined as I was to land a job at C&W after graduating from college, I knew eventually I had to create something that was all my own.

Coming from a family of entrepreneurs, I had always wanted to start, operate, and own my own company. My mother and father were both entrepreneurs at heart, and I absorbed so many lessons about self-sufficiency from watching their efforts in a variety of endeavors. My post-graduation summer in New York at my father's residential real estate office also added color to what I had studied and learned about the business at CU-Boulder, where I earned a business degree with an emphasis in real estate.

I decided to join C&W to learn the business, meet some of the right people, and make some money in anticipation of eventually starting my own investment company. In many ways, my time there provided a hands-on MBA education that allowed me to practice multiple skills on a daily basis. The brokerage environment taught me how to hunt and kill, to learn the art of the deal, to create and maintain momentum, to value properties and increase their value, and a host of other valuable lessons. My experiences during this time provided an invaluable foundation for the business I was about to build.

I tried to be realistic about the cost of taking this big step. After being a successful broker for seven years, I thought I would take a small step backward in preparation for making a giant economic leap forward. I had saved up enough money to live for a year, and I told my wife at the time that I would start this venture, and if it wasn't successful after the first year, I would then return to being a commercial real estate broker for another firm.

The beginning years were extremely exhilarating, challenging, and stressful. As the only founder of my company with no outside investors, I had to be the "chief cook and bottle washer," as old timers used to say on the Western Slope. From selecting the office space, to picking out furniture and equipment, to naming the company, designing a logo, launching a website, and marketing our materials, I had to do it all. Embracing this much responsibility allowed me to control every detail of my new business, and I found all this decision making and constant juggling exhilarating.

While launching the firm, I also had to pursue properties and secure investment deals, personally handwrite and sign all the checks, complete the accounting, and organize all forms, legal requirements, and records. Starting a new business is all-consuming and demands constant vigilance to avoid anything slipping through the cracks. The load was overwhelming most of the time, and looking back, I'm glad I was in my 20's when I launched Northstar and able to provide the time, focus, energy, and resiliency required by my new venture. As exhausting as it was, the process was also exciting—I wouldn't trade it for the world!

WHAT I WISH I'D KNOWN

Nothing can perfectly prepare you for becoming an entrepreneur and new business owner, other than a desire to learn from others and a willingness to invest all of the resources at your disposal.

Today, people often look at what we've achieved at Northstar Commercial Partners or see evidence of success in my lifestyle, and assume it all came easy. Many assume I inherited the business or had family wealth to invest when we first started. Others imply that I'm lucky and just happened to create the right business at the right time. While I understand their assumptions, the truth is that it took a tremendous amount of self-sacrifice, sweat equity, and sheer determination for Northstar to succeed, and it still does to this day.

While I would never deny that I'm incredibly blessed, I know that those blessings required an investment of myself into every facet of my business' operation. It's one thing to start a company and another to keep it operational and successful through good times as well as hard times. There's a good reason that the stats for business longevity and success are so low, with over 50% failing in the first year. Survival can be tough and requires focus and contribution on a daily basis.

I've learned so many lessons as an entrepreneur, with the most important ones often being learned the hard way—from firsthand experience. While sharing those lessons throughout this entire book, I've identified 20 lessons I wish I had known 20 years ago before I launched Northstar. I suspect the outcome of our success would be no different, but I might have saved some time, energy, and money along the way if I'd known then what I know now.

So I share these with you in hopes that you can learn from them and apply them in your own unique way in pursuit of building your own company or new venture. I'll save the other lessons for the chapters to come, but these are the most important ones that I wish someone would have shared with me all those years ago. Make them your own, use them to help you build something that will last, and ignore them at your own peril!

ENTREPRENEURSHIP 101

1. ***Know your reasons.*** Clearly determine why you want to be an entrepreneur and business owner, and write these down. Now print them and put them somewhere you can see them daily or refer to them frequently.
2. ***Identify your motives.*** After identifying your reasons for proceeding as an entrepreneur, assess your motives and ambitions. Are your reasons more about your needs or meeting the needs

of others? Some of the best companies seek to meet an unmet need in society, one that is compelling and beneficial to others. If you're motivated by the desire to serve others in some way, then you're more likely to succeed than if you're only promoting yourself and your personal success.

3. ***Balance strengths and weaknesses.*** Determine what your best skills are, and try to hire others with the skills that you don't have, or that are not the best use of your time, energy, and attention. In the beginning, most entrepreneurs have to "do it all," but the most successful ones focus on their strengths, identify their deficits and tasks that drain them, and have others make those contributions.

4. ***Commit to the cost.*** Are you willing to sacrifice virtually everything in your life to launch your new venture? Being an entrepreneur will demand your time, talent, and resources unlike most any other job or role you may have encountered. You must count the cost and realize what you will be forced to give up, at least the first year, if you're serious about creating a new business.

5. ***Face your fears.*** Decide if it is scarier for you to start a business, or never start one at all. If the latter, you will be more willing to do what it takes. If the former, identify what in particular scares you about launching your startup.

6. ***Know what you need.*** Determine if you're the kind of person who depends on security, needs a set schedule, and requires a predictable lifestyle. If you know you need any of these, let alone all three, then the challenges you face as an entrepreneur may be compounded.

7. ***Accept the risks.*** Are you willing to take risks, and if so, are you willing to gamble your financial security on your endeavor's fu-

ture success? You must come to terms with the very real possibility that you could lose everything invested in your new venture. Every day, an entrepreneur puts their name, reputation, money, and future on the line.

8. ***Prepare for the unpredictable.*** Launching a business always takes more time, energy, and money than you expect. Be prepared for this. Create margins for yourself in all of these areas so that you can handle the inevitable, unexpected demands that will arise.

9. ***Define your brand of success.*** Determine how you define success and be as specific as possible. Imagine yourself one year, three years, five years from the time you start your business—what does it look like for you to be at the top? What goals will you have achieved? Whether they're personal, financial, social, cultural or more, identify the targets you want to hit if you move forward with your launch. Be brutally honest with yourself, not pessimistic but as realistic as possible about the struggles, challenges, and obstacles you will likely face.

10. ***Identify the kind of entrepreneur you are.*** Are you a visionary, a starter, or an executer? Rarely, are entrepreneurs all three types, which becomes more apparent as a company grows. Knowing your natural style of leadership empowers you to address blind spots and anticipate vulnerabilities in your business.

11. ***Always be mindful of cash flow.*** The best time to ask for lines of credit, are when you do not need the money. The worst time to ask, is when you really need it for survival.

12. ***Hire the right people.*** Add value by hiring those team members who can fill in your weaknesses, the ones who take your organization to a higher level. Do not be intimidated by those who

may be more intelligent than you, especially in certain areas/facets. Your job as the entrepreneur is to define the idea, secure the best people, and implement. High tides raise all boats, and you will be better for surrounding yourself with a room of dedicated employees who are better and different than you in some ways.

13. *Start smart.* Try to limit the amount of personal guarantees on debt and services that you need, but understand that these are often required when starting a new venture.

14. *Accept the ebb and flow of personnel.* Don't take it personally when employees quit or move on. They may have personal life changes, or they may not share your vision and commitment. Each departure provides an opportunity to hire someone even more talented or better qualified.

15. *Include your employees in the interviewing process* for new hires. They can weed out the first cut of potential candidates, allowing you to pick from the top handful of candidates. If you have created a culture of achievement, accountability, and opportunity, then your staff will only want fellow "A Team" players on the field with them; otherwise, they will have to pick up their slack.

16. *Cover your assets.* Always use limited liability legal structures for your business to protect you from personal liability. While you hope your new business will be successful, you don't want to it to ruin you financially for the rest of your life.

17. *Guard your golden eggs.* Sign your own checks and oversee the accounting department as you grow. Your new venture's financial health is the proverbial hen house and should be guarded against foxes, both inside and outside, at all times.

18. *Practice attitude alchemy.* You will be told "no" more times than you can count because there are always critical naysayers

in this world. Listen and learn when appropriate, but don't allow them to limit you, discourage you, or change your vision. Use their critiques and negativity as opportunities to strengthen your ideas and improve your business. Focus on turning their negative energy into your fuel for positive growth.

19. *Stay humble.* Be willing to do any and every job in your company. You are not above or below anyone in the company you create. No matter how profitable, successful, or prominent your business becomes, you must remain humble if you wish to continue to grow and evolve with cultural changes.

20. *Be proactive rather than reactive* as much as possible. Life throws curve balls to us all, and the more you can anticipate and avoid certain problems and pitfalls rather than suffering through them with no preparation, the stronger you will be.

There's nothing quite as exhilarating as starting and growing your own company. If your experience is like mine, then I hope someday you will look back with wonderment that you were able to build it, pride that it is has lasted, and joy in anticipation of where it's going. Remember, very few people ever start their own business, and even fewer sustain it beyond the first year. Even fewer still are the ones to make it beyond year five.

You can do it, though, if you're willing to fail without ever giving up and to succeed without ever letting go. Learn as much as possible as you can every step of the way. No matter how many times the wild horse of your new business might try to throw you, hold on for dear life, get back in the saddle when you fall off, and always enjoy the ride!

CHAPTER 6

TIME AND TIDES— ECONOMIC EBBS AND FLOWS

"A creative economy is the fuel of magnificence."

--RALPH WALDO EMERSON

I love to fish. It's more than just a hobby—it's part of who I am and what I love to do. Like any passionate pursuit or personal interest, fishing has taught me a great deal about investing. As a saltwater fisherman, I can't help but liken the inevitable economic shifting back and forth to the ocean tides. Each day, the tide gradually rises and falls, due to the gravitational pull of the moon. Both the outgoing and incoming tides create opportunities for catching fish, but one must use different bait, techniques, and strategy based on the timing, location, and strength of the tide.

As someone who has been working to provide for himself since I left home at age 17, I've experienced the rise and fall of the economy, the fluctuations of markets, as well as the ups and downs with my own company. Change is a constant, and though we often fear change and long for what's familiar and predictable, dramatic economic changes also create opportunities. Whether an economy is growing stronger or falling in a downward spiral, its movement always creates opportunities for investment.

TIDAL WAVES

The worst time for fishing is in a slack tide, when the water is still and fish are generally not active. Fish need to feed, and they like movement, which usually brings in an assortment of species and smaller fish. Tidal fluctuations carry food out to sea from the inland areas, whereas an incoming tide will draw in food from the sea to the more shallow areas.

Though you can predict the tide, you cannot always predict exactly what the fish will eat, and even the placement of the line and bait have to be presented correctly, at the right depth, with the proper slack in the line, proper size of bait, with a natural appearance. Depending on how you look at it, fish are either smart or somewhat lazy. They like to place themselves in the best position to have the food come to them, and the bigger fish are able to place themselves in the prime positions.

While fishing, you have to figure out how to place the right bait or fly—with the look, size, and texture of what the fish want to feed on—at just the right position, height, and location on or in the water. Otherwise, the fish will not be interested in what you're offering to entice them. While it may sound obvious, don't forget that even if the fish don't seem to be biting, the only way you have a chance to catch one is if you first have a line in the water. Otherwise, you're guaranteed not to catch anything at all!

WATCHING AND WAITING

Sometimes when the fish aren't biting, you need to switch it up and try a different bait, a heavier sinker, or none at all, to attract the attention of a ten-pound sea bass or red snapper. Other times, you may need to change locations and go upstream or downstream, wade into deeper water or turn back to the shore. Where the tide may be slack in one area, it may be coming in or going out in another area given the time it takes to move. Naturally, you should look closely and head to the area where the water is moving, to adapt to the current situation and conditions.

In commercial real estate, the change in markets and economies often creates great buying, holding, or selling opportunities. I'm a believer that you can make a good or bad investment in either a bull or bear market. This essential strategy overall, however, is simply to keep some lines in the water at all times, trolling for the highest quality fish. I like it when people make over generalizations about a market, when they state things like "the economy is too hot—there are no good deals," or "we're too far along in the investment cycle with no values remaining," or "the economy is horrible, and it is a bad time to buy anything as it will continue to fall," or "there's no hope for the foreseeable future."

Such statements by prognosticators tend to become self-fulfilling prophecies from my experience. If you make such proclamations and believe there are no good deals out there to buy, guess what? You have placed blinders on your eyes and limited your perception to spot great deals even when they're right in front of you! I've bought some of my best investments in the worst of markets when everyone around me said that none were to be found. I've also made some incredible investments in the midst of great markets that others told me were saturated. And, obviously, I've invested at times during times of market flux, sometimes exceeding a 600% return on equity!

If I don't keep casting my lines into the water, though, I'm guaranteed to miss out. The ocean tides are absolute realities and provide a pace and rhythm to a natural cycle. Similarly, the economy ebbs and flows and reveals opportunities to succeed if we're watching and waiting.

TRUST YOUR GUT

If you want to be a shrewd investor, be open-minded and maintain a respect for the ebbing and flowing of the market. Once you identify a deal you want to invest in, don't hesitate! Timing is indeed everything. The more experience you gain, the more naturally you can spot the rhythm of investment cycles in certain industries and companies.

Listen and learn from others, but ultimately trust your gut. You are becoming an expert every bit as qualified, perhaps more, than so many of the financial gurus out there giving advice and making pitches. If you think about it, isn't it curious that the majority of economists, business commentators, and financial planners have not become billionaires themselves?

If these people were so good with their insights and predictions, then they should have become wealthy executing on their own ideas, that they shouldn't still need a job commenting on the present market conditions or predicting the future! I appreciate their perspectives, but understand that they are not always experts, and rarely are they 100% correct. Markets and economies move and undulate, and even though the Dow, Nasdaq, and/or any other market index may be doing X or Y, it doesn't mean that the entire market is going to follow.

At my company, I have made it clear that we're not buying the entire market. Instead, we're buying one specific asset, in a specific location, at a specific price, with specific attributes, challenges, and benefits within a particular market. We're executing on this one deal, in the context of an overall market. All assets are not created equal, and though it's valuable to evaluate a market and understand past performance, averages and trends, it's our job to execute on this particular asset to create a profit for our investors.

We're not always successful, and there's always risk involved, but our performance has exceeded the average market returns for several decades. Though past performance does not guarantee future success, we will continue to remain focused in our approach to creating value. It's not so much a specific strategy as much an attitude of overall investment.

GO FISH

Like all entrepreneurs who launch a new business, I never desired to create a mediocre company when I started Northstar Commercial Partners. If anything, I wanted to stand out and to be distinct from all the other firms and companies with whom we would be competing. I wanted to create a superior company that consistently competes head-to-head with others, and wins. That was my goal then, and it remains my goal today. Consequently, we will continue to search for great opportunities regardless of current market conditions because we firmly believe that there are always fish no matter how the tides may be flowing.

Ask anyone who loves fishing, and you'll discover that their passion includes more than simply catching fish. Nor is their joy dependent on the number of fish they caught, or their catch's length or weight. Fishing is an experience that transcends any one expedition or fish caught that day. Fishing is about savoring the entire process of preparing, studying, researching, and equipping. It's about the joy that comes from feeling the sun on your face while standing in knee-deep waters casting your line toward a blue-lined horizon. It's about enjoying the fulfillment that comes from pursuing a goal over and over again, learning and maturing each time.

Investing is the same way. It requires patience and passion beyond any one deal. It's about more than just making a profit or finding a hidden gem no one else spotted at the time. It's the competitive thrill of taking a risk on a hunch or learning from a loss you didn't see coming. Accept the adventure of investing and you will not only learn from the process, but you will grow from what you learn. So go fish!

CHAPTER 7

THE MOGULS— OBSTACLES AND OPPORTUNITIES

"Opportunities to find deeper powers within ourselves come when life seems most challenging."

--JOSEPH CAMPBELL

Living in Colorado for most of my life, I am an avid skier. There's nothing quite like skiing down a snow-covered mountain with the sun shining on your face and the blue sky unfolding above. I love the whoosh of skis on powder, the evergreens edging the forests beyond the slopes, and the sting of cold wind on red cheeks. Building up speed on a steep descent may be the closest thing to flying I'll ever experience.

As a skier becomes more adept, he or she begins to tackle moguls, or as many call them, "bumps." Some mogul runs are very technical, and exceedingly steep, resembling a vertical blade embossed by ridges of ice. Unlike a nice, groomed blue run that allows you to enjoy a smooth ride all the way down to the bottom, moguls require constant attention, concentrated effort, split-second timing, and skill. Even after mastering these snow bumps, you can still fall, leaving both your body and your ego bruised.

In more extreme cases, a bad fall can lead to a hospital visit followed by months of reconstructive surgery and physical therapy for a blown knee or broken limb. Fractured ribs are quite common, and some mogul-enthusiasts damage their vertebrae as well. Obviously, skiing moguls is not for the faint of heart and appeals more to thrill seekers. But if you enjoy the outdoors and want to test your mind, heart, and body, then this might be for you.

LEARNING TO SKI

As an entrepreneur, I believe conducting business is often like learning to ski and then tackling the moguls. If you're the type of person too intimated to put on a pair of skis and ride the mountain, then you might not enjoy the thrilling ups and downs of being an entrepreneur. While I enjoy cross-country skiing, and appreciate the incredible strength and power it requires to sustain the trek, it's not nearly as exciting as downhill. If you're more of a cross-country type, you can certainly find many businesses that provide slow, steady rewards for the hard work you invest. But don't settle for slow and steady before you at least attempt to run the moguls!

Once you're committed to launching your new business or tackling the ski slopes, you have to make sure you're adequately equipped. You don't have to have the best skis or the latest outfits from designer brands, but you do want to make sure you have decent skis for the mountain you're about to attempt. And it's no fun being cold and wet, which are both inevitable realities when skiing long enough, so you want some kind of protection from the elements. Similarly, entrepreneurs need to be equipped with enough time, energy, product, human resources, and capital to at least complete their first run.

Once you're suited up and in your ski boots, then it's time to assess your ability and experience. Many people love to ski but few begin with as much skill and ability as they often think they have. Try to be realistic and humble about the experience you already have as well as honest if you don't have any experience at all. There's no shame in being a beginner—the problem is when you're overly confident in areas where you lack experience. In business as well as skiing, you need to know what you don't know.

Let's assume you're just beginning. As you put on skis for the first time, you will start off on a "bunny slope," a green run for the most basic of beginners without much incline. Nonetheless, when you're first learning to ski, even the bunny slope can seem scary and frustrating as you experience numerous falls. Then, as you learn how to maintain balance and master moving your skis into the fundamental positions that instructors often call "French fries" and "pizza slices," you start to increase skill and gain confidence.

Soon, that bunny slope no longer offers any challenge and begins to look more like you're launching pad than an actual ski slope. So you move on to green slopes with more incline before graduating to blue runs where sometimes you can meet moguls for the first time. Then you get a few blue runs under your belt, and you're ready to attempt some "jumps on bumps" and confront those intentional obstacles in your path. This is your progression as you gain the strength and stamina required to hit the bumps hard as you come to enjoy the thrill more and more.

Going down the mountain allows you to experience the different challenges of life, with the bumps representing the challenges that arise as you increase speed and gain more control. Once you hit one bump and overcome it, the next bump is right behind it. You can never just assume your run will follow a smooth trail, and even when you're anticipating bumps along the way, they may still catch you off guard and send you flying to the ground. Like looking down the slope and seeing only white on white, you have to assume bumps are in front of you even when you can't see them.

PICK YOUR LINES

Once you have mastered the basics of business and of skiing, then the fun begins. Often you begin at the top of a hill, surveying the landscape below before deciding which run you want to take. With your selection in your sights, you push off and start down the mountain, eager for the thrilling ride ahead while also a bit nervous about any unexpected obstacles in your path. Once you're on your way, you usually know immediately whether you chose the right run for your ability.

If you start off too fast, you may quickly fall, or try to over correct, and then "biff out" in a crash of white powder. When this happens, your ski buddies will likely laugh, grateful that it happened to you before it happens to them. They will watch your spectacular crash with awe and amusement, followed by more laughter. But then you pick yourself up, take a deep breath, and push off to start again. You may even learn to laugh with them the next time you—or they—take a spill.

As you grow in competence, you gradually realize that the key to mastering the bumps is to pick your line and stick with it, while adapting and changing it up as required. Agility and speedy reflexes also help. You must learn to control and exert muscles in your body you may not use for any other activities. Core strength is essential if you're going to maintain your balance while racing at speeds that can easily reach up to forty miles per hour on advanced slopes.

The only way to pick your line and stay focused is to continually adapt.

This strategy holds true in our business lives as well: If we don't pick our lines and stick with our direction, we will soon be distracted. Then we can easily allow our skis to get too high on the bump, get crossed, or extend too far in front of us—with each error leading to the same crashing result. On the slopes and in the markets, there's a magic balance between leaning into the mountain and monitoring your speed. You must practice keeping your legs and body nimble and flexible to take the hits when you jump, using your poles to stake each bump and push off into the next. Otherwise, you slow your descent even as you stress your body beyond what your muscles can bear.

Every once in a while, you may need to stop on the mountain and catch your breath, let your muscles recover, and have an energy bar or other snack to ensure you have enough fuel to make it to the bottom. You also need to stop and enjoy the view, soaking in the stunning peaks, cascading slopes, and open-handed sky. The exhilaration of watching your breath cloud the cold air and feeling your heart pound is simply unbeatable. Never forget to enjoy it, to look at how far you've come and the terrain you still want to tackle.

Each of these tasks is important in business as well. In order to reach your goal successfully, you must use the right techniques to maintain control, monitor your speed, slow down and even pause at times, and replenish personal fuel as well as capital for your business. Most importantly, you must remember to take in the view and enjoy the process. Look back at where you started and how far you've come and then refocus on where you're going before resuming your run. Spend a moment reflecting on what you're learning and what you will do differently on the next run—and the next deal.

JUMP BY JUMP

Like an advanced mogul run, life tends to be relentless. When you address one bump, you can usually survive it and not regret choosing the trail you're on. But then after subsequent bumps leave you dizzy and unbalanced, then you may need to stop and reconsider. Maybe it's time to switch to another trail and decrease your velocity. Perhaps you were not as ready as you thought you were to face so many obstacles in your path at such a rapid pace. You might even decide that you prefer cross-country skiing—or even snowshoeing—after all!

Recessions and market changes can present more challenging bumps, and may even lead you into double black diamond territory, the designation for the most advanced and challenging trails on the mountain. If you take these challenges head on, and refuse to be intimidated by them, then you learn not only to overcome them but also to trust yourself in the midst of such dangerous situations. You gain confidence and learn to identify your strengths and your weaknesses as well as the parts of the path that give you the most trouble.

You may even discover that you love the satisfaction from giving all you've got and conquering the obstacles thrown in your path. In fact, it is often these truly challenging experiences that stimulate your senses, test your abilities, and teach you the most—about yourself, about the market, and about life.

In business and in life, there will always be times where the terrain looks tough, when you look down and momentarily experience vertigo, afraid that you may fall headfirst. But in those moments, always remember that you only have to take each mogul as it comes, one at a time, bump by bump, and jump by jump.

The experience is always worth it because each run, like each deal, has much to teach you. Some will go faster and smoother than you ever imagined, while others will leave you fallen and frustrated. Once you experience the thrill of skiing moguls, then you understand the way obstacles in your path can become opportunities for greatness.

CHAPTER 8

DIAMONDS IN THE ROUGH

"Better a diamond with a flaw than a pebble without one."

--CHINESE PROVERB

Commercial real estate investing can take many forms. From core, to value-add, to opportunistic, different investors flock to different investment alternatives and product types, often based on size, risk, return, or availability. Most career investors often specialize in particular areas, markets, or unique kinds of properties. As someone focused on achieving above market returns, I have done this by pursuing properties that are the "diamonds in the rough."

While the phrase has become a cliché, if you contemplate the origin of this maxim—literally, from mining the world's most precious gemstones—you then understand how potential value is identified, fully realized, and enhanced. Arguably, the value of any commodity is in the eye of the beholder, or in the case of property, in the vision of the prospective tenant or buyer. The best diamond merchants know that it's worth the effort to search for gemstones that others might overlook or undervalue. Diamonds in the rough can be an investor's best friend!

BURIED TREASURE

For centuries, diamonds have been sought for their brilliant luster and sparkling clarity, especially compared to other rocks, minerals, and gems. Similar to mining for gold or other precious resources, diamond hunters spend years researching specific geographic areas that are likely to yield such treasure. Once an area of focus is determined, even more time is spent sifting through a lot of soil, looking for a hint of a sparkle.

This search is obviously very labor intensive, and a tremendous amount of soil and rock need to be excavated to find these precious stones, the ones that actually hold value. Similar to looking for the proverbial needle in a haystack, diamond miners can spend days, weeks, or months culling the dust for a speck of glitter. Once actual diamonds have been identified in the target area, then the search becomes more intensive. Eventually, a few diamonds in their rough, natural state are extracted, the result of thousands of years of pressure on coal deep within the earth.

These jagged rocks and mineral beds look nothing like the smooth, sparkling stones in glass jewelers' cases or around people's necks and fingers. Basically, these are just lumpy rocks with potential! And this last word is key, because with any natural resource, the true value lies within and must be extracted to reveal its worth.

Real estate investment works in a similar way.

You have to know how to spot buried treasure and start looking in the right area for it. Many investors cannot see the diamonds in the rough, choosing instead to focus on finished high-end properties, usually just as a status symbol of their buying power or "good taste." These properties are the finished diamonds, assets that people can already see the value in buying, ones that often command market or above-market prices. These might be historic, even iconic properties sometimes associated with a particular event or famous person.

For example, these might include an office building that was designed by a famous architect or hosted an important event. When these make a splash in the market, they usually have been renovated already, perhaps starting as another investor's diamond in the rough or labor of love. Other status properties are often the latest-and-greatest, the work of a world-renowned designer featuring distinct features that give it a specific identity. The Shed at Hudson Yards in New York City or Denver's Wells Fargo Center, which most of us locals call the "Cash Register Building" because of its striking resemblance, are examples of these kinds of buildings.

These dramatic properties are great purchases if you're motivated by ego, status, or sentiment, but aren't your best choice if you want to make a higher-than-average return on your investment. The best value in commercial real estate is to find a rough diamond that others haven't recognized as such or else consider too much work to realize.

Mining these hidden gems is only the beginning, of course, because then a jeweler must take the dirty, lumpy, jagged rock and transform it into an extraordinary, brilliant sparkler. This process requires time and effort, including the all-important selection of properties with the most unrealized potential for the price. Just as not all stones are worth the investment required to produce a marketable diamond, so it goes with properties.

Once these rough-diamond properties have been selected, then the time-intensive stage of development begins. Skilled diamond cutters know how to take an existing stone and refine it to its highest and best value. Each stone presents unique features and attributes, and if the cutter does their job well, then a spectacular diamond emerges.

ALL SHAPES AND SIZES

At Northstar, we focus on acquiring these diamonds in the rough as the heart of our investment strategy. Our purchases are usually vacant or distressed commercial real estate properties that we acquire in one of three ways: from financial institutions that foreclosed on them; from companies that do not need the facilities any longer and/ or want to increase cash flow and transfer liability off their balance sheet; and by municipalities and other property owners that want to turn a blighted vacant property into an attractive resource for their community. These assets come in all shapes and sizes, and we have to determine what is the highest and best use for that particular asset, similar to the diamond cutter.

Often we acquire office, retail, or industrial buildings to reposition them for their originally intended uses, and other times we will redevelop them for educational and entrepreneurial purposes that offer the maximum benefit to the surrounding community stakeholders. We ask, "What's the highest and best use here—regardless of the condition and original intended purpose of this property?"

Other institutional investors are usually focused and required to buy a specific asset class, by their mandates. Consequently, if you are an office real estate investment trust (REIT) for example, you have to buy cash-flowing office properties without exercising creative control over what it could become. As I see it, these investors paint themselves into a corner by setting parameters of what they can and cannot buy, and thus their returns trend back to the average market norms for that particular asset class.

Obviously, each specialized investor attempts to create value through different management styles, capital deployment, and redevelopment strategies, but they're often forced to chase after the same limited pool of properties. Northstar, however, is designed to remain nimble in order to move easily in and out of various markets, product types, and final uses.

Our goal is to buy the diamond in the rough at 50% or less of replacement-cost value and then to reposition that asset to its highest and best use, which then creates the highest return on invested money for our capital partners. This alignment of interests, in trying to secure the highest return for our investors while also having a positive social impact for the community, allows us to seek out above-market results. This strategy produces more profit for investors and a greater positive impact for the community, thus yielding win-win outcomes for stakeholders.

THE 4 C'S OF DIAMOND PROPERTIES

If you've ever shopped for the perfect diamond, then you know all stones are not created equal. They may appear the same, even identical, to the naked eye, but ultimately, they each have distinct differences in quality. These are usually called the four C's: carat weight, cut, color, and clarity. These qualities combined then determine a stone's ultimate value. Obviously, properties are not all the same nor are they necessarily what they appear to be. Expert inspections are crucial before purchasing a building in order to ensure it meets basic criteria. While you want to identify a diamond in the rough, you don't want to end up with a cubic zirconia, a synthetically made imitation with very little value!

Most jewelers know that a diamond's carat weight often determines how it will be cut into smaller stones. While customers often assume bigger is better, this is not always the case, in gemstones or in properties. Square footage determines many aspects of a property's potential, but it must be considered within the context of other facets, such as location, work required, and relationship to the community.

The cut of a diamond releases its sparkle, revealing the lustrous fire within the stone. Consequently, the cutter studies the stone in order to make the most flattering cut to showcase its qualities. Some examples include a princess cut, emerald cut, or solitaire. Similarly, commercial properties may need to be reconfigured, moving offices, conference rooms, cubicles, and media rooms to create a more natural flow or to suit prospective tenants.

The color of a diamond sounds obvious, but apparently there are subtle differences in mineral composition that result in some diamonds appearing whiter and others more yellow or golden. The color of the stone cannot be changed naturally so the jeweler attempts to complement the diamond's color with a flattering setting. Properties often need flattering styles of design and décor to match the building's architectural style and period details. Some design elements can be changed and updated and others are too costly or risk compromising its structural integrity. Knowing the difference is both art and science.

Finally, a diamond's clarity is often what one notices first since clarity determines the amount of light passing through and reflected by the facets of the stone. A purity in clarity may result in a small diamond being valued much higher than a larger, yet flawed or cloudy stone. For properties, we sometimes talk about a building having "good bones," meaning its key structural components are sound and solid. If a property's basic features are excellent, then cosmetic fixes will be easy. On the other hand, if the building lacks diamond-like clarity, then no amount of renovation may increase its value.

READY TO WEAR

Our diamond cutting and refining process happens as we improve the chosen assets to maximize their full potential. We often refer to this as removing the "hair." This process may include demolishing the interior to open it up, increasing the ceiling height, painting and re-carpeting the premises, building out interior space to be more functional, removing environmental contamination, and replacing major components such as the HVAC system or roof.

Our overhaul infuses new life into the previous space, illuminating a vision that previous owners never realized and that subsequent occupants won't be able to see without our construction and design experience. Just as a rough diamond often looks better after it has been cut, polished, and set, our properties benefit from the same kind of improvements.

When prospective occupants or potential buyers can see that a building has been improved, they perceive that the entire property has a higher value. On the other hand, if they see holes in the walls, a leaking roof, worn carpets, and outdated fixtures, they will assume the entire building has been neglected and needs updating. Simply put, we remove the barriers to "yes" and work to remediate issues we would want addressed if we were occupying the space ourselves.

Removing the barriers to an easy "yes" is a very important concept. In order to finalize a lease, sale, or most any transaction, investors have to pay the way toward helping others see the beauty of the diamond they've uncovered. This principle reminds me of the Olympic Curling event. If you've ever seen this competition, then you know how important it is for the ice to be brushed and polished in order to remove any obstacles or debris that might create unwanted friction. Our process of cleaning, clearing, and clarifying our property paves the way for a smooth transaction.

In commercial real estate investment, most tenants and buyers do not want a "project." They want a turnkey space or updated building that meets their needs in a reasonable way, at a reasonable if not bargain price so they can stay focused on their primary business. Imagine shopping in a jewelry store and only seeing uncut and unpolished stones in the case. Such unfinished gems, just like unimproved properties, are not attractive as most customers want something ready right now.

Therefore, the more that we can make the building or space move-in ready, often to their specific needs or requirements, the more likely we are to close the deal on our diamond-like property. People need and want space so they can focus on their business operations, and the easier that you can make this decision for them, the more likely they will be to commit to you.

By buying the diamond in the rough at lower than market values, improving it to make it look attractive and inhabitable, and removing the barriers to occupancy, the more financially successful you will be. If you do this well, then you will be able to sell your finished, sparkling diamonds in the marketplace, knowing you have pleased your customers by realizing the potential of your beautiful gem.

CHAPTER 9

PASSION + PURPOSE = PROFESSION

"Vocation is the place where our deep gladness meets the world's deep need."

--FREDERICK BUECHNER

Work helps us create value and meaning in our lives. As an integral component to our existence, work also allows us to acquire the items we need or want according to the lifestyle we choose. Humans have worked in one form another since the beginning of time, and our desire to produce order from chaos seems crucial to the way we interact with the world. I'm convinced we were created to create.

At first, we work for basic needs and survival, but as we meet these essential requirements, we then work to achieve. This is the basic premise of psychologist Abraham Maslow's hierarchy of needs, asserted in his seminal 1943 article "A Theory of Human Motivation," which asserts that we desire more, even as we achieve more. According to his model, life is like a pyramid where, at the base, we first pursue biological and physiological needs such as food, water, shelter, air, and sleep. Needs related to safety and survival come at the next level followed by needs related to belonging and love. Personal esteem needs come next with self-actualization, the need to reach one's full potential and experience fulfillment, at the top of the pyramid.

With so many of the lower tiers completed, many people still engage in what our Founding Fathers called "the pursuit of happiness." Even after you've secured decent economic means, which is relative to each person and their goals and desires, you still yearn to do something of meaning and significance with your life, rather than merely existing or consuming.

Accepting work as a foundational part of human existence, you might as well find a way to enjoy what you do rather than going through the motions in a job that leaves you bored and unfulfilled. Perhaps I'm oversimplifying the options, but as I see it you have a choice: make your work something you enjoy or accept a painful struggle with futility.

Some people believe they don't have a choice, but we always have choices. In actuality, you are the architect of your life. Embracing this mindset allows you to be proactive or intentionally reactive in your decision-making. Once you own responsibility for your life's choices, then turning your personal passions into your profession becomes mandatory. When you use your skills, talents, abilities, and experience to make a living in ways that fulfill you, then your entire journey becomes much more exciting, rewarding, and that word we often think of from childhood: fun.

TIP OF THE ICEBERG

As an entrepreneur at heart, I know starting, owning, and operating a national commercial real estate investment firm is part of my life's calling. Though each of us can have challenging days or difficult times, there's nothing quite like waking up every morning excited to go to work. While I'm in the shower or getting ready for the day, I often think about goals for that day or new solutions to ongoing puzzles. Typically, I send myself an email reminder about these ideas so I can capitalize on them once I get to the office.

As someone who can make decisions immediately upon receiving adequate information, without the need for approval from a board of directors, other executives, or outside investors, I can implement my plans promptly. This mobility allows Northstar Commercial Partners to be nimble, quick, and responsive. By listening to my subconscious mind and acting upon the innovations and solutions it generates, I encourage and empower it to create even more. This may sound strange, but I'm a believer!

Thoughts from our minds compare to an iceberg at sea: What we often "see" is the just the tip, with over three-quarters of our potential, solutions, and capabilities submerged below the surface. If you encourage the continuous flow of thoughts and ideas, and draw from the deeper creative well within your mind, then you will untap a wellspring of connections, innovations, and possibilities you might never realize otherwise.

The more that you listen to these ideas, act upon them, and celebrate the successes from them, the more your mind will work to push them up to your consciousness. Obviously, not every idea should be acted upon, or will result in success, but you should still listen to them, compare them to other options, and act upon them if they seem feasible. Unfortunately, most people aren't willing to practice this kind of creative thinking and active risk-taking. It's not just thinking outside the box. It's learning to *practice* thinking outside the box and acting upon it that's often the key to lasting success.

PAY ATTENTION

Each of us has a very unique set of backgrounds, experiences, thoughts, and goals. There is *no one else* on planet earth, whether in its entire history, present, or future, with your *exact* blend of personality, purpose, and passion. Truly think about that for a minute, and let it sink fully into your psyche.

You are unlike anyone else on the planet—this is your greatest asset!

There is no one with your exact combination of these ingredients, and thus your unique ability to act upon them. Given this, you are uniquely positioned to think about an idea, act upon a strategy, or implement a transformational concept that literally no one else can do. Even if another person thought of your particular idea, they would not act upon it the same way. Your unique make-up enables you to execute on each new idea differently than another person with different experiences, goals, and abilities.

This realization first dawned on me when I was a commercial real estate broker with Cushman & Wakefield of Colorado for seven years. As I was constantly searching for a deal, which either meant securing a tenant representation agreement with a company or getting a listing agreement to lease or sell a building for an owner, I would drive down the road focused on making the most of my time and abilities. Driving by an office building in the course of my day, I'd look for a moving truck out front or a parking lot with only a few cars in it. Then, I'd pull over and look up the Ownership and Encumbrance Report (known as O&E in the industry) for that property to identify the owners. Based mostly on my first impression and gut instinct, I'd call the owners to see if they needed a broker to list the building for sale or lease.

Other times, I'd read the newspaper and learn that a company was having financial trouble or that another firm was growing rapidly due to a new contract they secured. Armed with this information, I called on them to see if I could help them get rid of existing space to downsize or secure new space to grow. These aren't just tricks of the trade or personal preferences about how to land a deal. My point is that I trained myself to *pay attention* both to *external details* and information as well as to *internal instincts*. Rather than just noticing something casually, I became a student focused on a mission.

The vast majority of people who drove by those buildings or skimmed those newspaper articles either didn't notice or didn't care enough to follow up, or couldn't have extracted value from it even if they did, as this wasn't their profession. While a few brokers might have landed a deal this way, the vast majority seemed to wait for deals to come to them, or were not focused on constantly searching for opportunities. Although the brokerage community was highly competitive, I may have been the only person with the knowledge and capability to act upon that particular opportunity that I happened to identify, out of millions of people in Colorado at the time.

You have the same unique opportunities waiting for you! Right now, even as you're reading these words, you could be the only person on the entire planet who could act upon a specific idea or cause and make it a reality. If you allow them to guide you, your experiences, capabilities, and skills will lead you to moments where you alone see what needs to be done.

BEST IN, BEST OUT

Our human minds are constantly thinking, putting ideas and concepts together, analyzing, and making combinations and thoughts that no other mind has conceived. If you train your mind to think about opportunities, and then actually work to implement them, the end result will often exceed your imagination. As you enjoy the pleasure and fulfillment of creating and innovating new ideas, your mind will use this as positive reinforcement to generate even more big ideas.

On the other hand, if you ignore or reject these ideas, or fail to follow through after noting them, then your mind will not offer up many inventive solutions. If you keep telling yourself that it's not worth the trouble to attempt new solutions or to step out in faith toward a seemingly impossible goal, then you train your mind to accept self-imposed—and debilitating—limitations. Expectations cut both ways, and when you don't expect to succeed, you usually won't.

The old computer data adage about "garbage in, garbage out" still holds true when referring to the data we allow into our minds. Our brains encompass even more sophisticated software than any computer so it's likely even more sensitive to positive and negative influence. Your "garbage data" might result from past psychological and emotional wounds, a negative attitude, lack of confidence, substance abuse, or addictive behavior that impedes your body's mastermind from operating at full creative capacity.

If you want to be successful, then you must filter what you put in your mind. You have to focus on constructive criticism instead of pessimistic possibilities, on praise instead of blame, and on strengths instead of weaknesses. You have to exercise your imagination regularly and devote hard work to executing what you envision. You have to fuel your body and your mind with the best if you want to be the best. Perhaps it's time to replace "garbage in, garbage out" with "best in, best out."

MIND OVER MATTER

Your mind helps determine what matters most to you. It's a magical moment when your limitlessly creative mind focuses on making your passions your profession. You have the double positive impact of having your passions enflamed by a mind that's constantly searching for ways to spark new possibilities for your profession. Once an idea catches, your passion becomes the fuel to illuminate new ways to work at what you love.

Exploring areas of keen interest, you become excited to channel your energy, attention, and time into creating a career that's more than just an occupation. Instead, it becomes your vocation, the calling on your life that infuses purpose into everything you do. Once you're motivated by your unique personal purpose and fueled by your deepest passions, work no longer seems like drudgery or tedium. You're no longer supporting someone else's dream because you have your own.

For most of my adult life, since I was a young teenager actually, I've worked more than 40 hours per week. I know this for a fact because in addition to the time I put in the office, meetings, and administrative work, I put that much more time into generating new and better ways to reach my goals. I'm constantly thinking about ways to improve my company, build up my staff, or execute on an existing or new investment. My ideas come throughout the day, from the time I wake up to the moment I fall asleep.

As they surface, I'm quick to act upon them for two reasons. First, I want to encourage my mind to create more ideas through the positive reinforcement we were just discussing. And, secondly, I also want to free up mental space for new and even better ideas. The more I can get them out and begin exploring how or when to implement them, the more momentum I can gain.

Develop your mind, follow your curiosity, and prepare to be surprised!

VOCATION IS VACATION

I truly love what I do for my profession, and there's not another business profession in this world that I'd rather have. Even if I won the lottery of millions or magically inherited billions, I would still do what I do. I love it that much!

There's nothing quite like the thrill of starting a company and building it for decades. The satisfaction that comes from spotting a diamond-in-the-rough property, buying it, cleaning and polishing it, and making a phenomenal return on our investment is unparalleled. The exhilaration comes not only from winning the investment game but also from making the process meaningful to others along the way.

This win-win includes helping my employees grow within the company, develop professionally, and earn a living to achieve their own goals and dreams for themselves and their families. My joy also comes from the blessing of giving back to communities and increasing both property values as well as personal values. At the end of the day, that's what drives me.

My passion is always to create value, to make a positive difference, and to live a life of meaning and purpose. Commercial real estate has allowed me to fulfill this passion in the form of my profession. Yours may be creating unique products and services, teaching and leading others, or inventing new technologies for improving lives. Whatever you're doing, I urge you to consider how to find the sweet spot where your passions, purpose, and profession can intersect.

If you do, you will never work another day in your life because your satisfaction will always outweigh your sacrifice. You may still be on a journey from your current job to your preferred passionate profession, but if you keep pursuing what you care most about in life, then you will move closer and closer to realizing your dreams. Focus on what gets you excited, what drives you, what you wish to be remembered for, and then figure out how you can make a profession out of it. Invest in a foundation of happiness and contentment by persevering toward your passions.

Let your vocation be your soul's vacation—one that lasts a life-time!

CHAPTER 10

THE SOCIAL CONTRACT OF POSITIVE IMPACT

"Since you get more joy out of giving joy to others, you should put a good deal of thought into the happiness that you are able to give."

--ELEANOR ROOSEVELT

Our life goals and personal purpose cannot be solely for our own benefit. We are all part of the global community of humanity. We are all called to serve one another and contribute to lasting improvement for each other and the entire human race. Though people need to fulfill their basic needs of food, shelter, and security, as these needs are met, they also long to fulfill their true meaning and purpose. We all want to believe that being here on this earth makes a difference to those around us—and to those who follow.

While monetary and financial goals are good to have in place, they cannot be the sole measuring stick of your life if you hope to be truly fulfilled and happy. If your primary aspiration is simply to make a lot of money, live in your dream home, and have others think you're important, then you're potentially setting yourself up for a huge letdown. Ask anyone who has pursued a life focused entirely on monetary success and material possessions, and if they're honest, they will reveal the hollow center at the core of their success.

ENOUGH IS NEVER ENOUGH

Research studies as well as personal experience reveal that enough is never enough. The more money you make, the more you will inevitably spend as your tastes, desires, and lifestyle expand to keep up with your income. The more you attain, the more you raise the bar to an even higher, ultimately unattainable level. It often happens without even trying. Simply put, if you have more, then you spend more.

You may think this is not the case for you, and perhaps it's not. But take a moment and honestly reflect on your life now compared to five, ten, or twenty years ago. How does what you made financially when you were younger stack up against what you're worth now? How many of the goals, possessions, or bucket-list items did you set for yourself that you've now achieved? Compared to what you wanted at the beginning of your adult life, what do you want now?

Humans were uniquely created, and part of our inherent identity requires us to seek meaning. In my first book, *The 7 Rings*, I explore the God-shaped void that exists within each of our hearts. This spiritual part of us seeks meaning and purpose, the kind of contentment in life that transcends dollars and cents. This meaning comes from being part of the human experience and understanding our spiritual worth.

Ultimately, we need to benefit the world in some way to find true fulfillment.

GENEROUS GRATITUDE

The social contract of positive impact means that whether you're setting goals for your profession or for your own personal pursuits, or a combination of both, you also have a responsibility to benefit others. Your life cannot just be about you. No one lives in a void, cut off from relationships and isolated from society. No matter our season or station of life, we all should consider the needs of others as well.

Some of the biggest blessings in this life are to see the needs of another, and then to help meet those needs in some positive way. Meeting those needs is not just about sharing financial resources, although that may indeed be part of the process. Meeting the needs of others is about giving your time, attention, energy, and ingenuity just as much as your money.

Just as you're uniquely positioned to spot opportunities where your passions and purpose can intersect for your profession, you're also uniquely qualified to see and meet the needs of others. Thinking creatively and being in the present moment apply here as well. The more you recognize and act upon the needs of others, the more your mind will think of ways to benefit others. The blessing and positive feelings that come from this service far outweigh that next deal, the big closing, or that status purchase.

When you have the ability to benefit another—without any financial reward—just because you can, the result is both empowering and euphoric. In my service to others through the years, I have benefited more by such service, than at times the benefit I have provided. The older I get, the more I appreciate how much pleasure it affords to give to others. It's not just our social contract—it's a privilege that fulfills us unlike any other.

While our act of service presumably helps someone else, in the process we become better people—humbler, more compassionate, and more generous. Often it's only when we take our eyes off our own lives that we realize how much we have. Giving makes us grateful. When we share life's blessings with those in need, we realize how much we tend to take for granted.

Our own problems diminish in light of seeing what so many people have to endure. This is not about measuring one's life or problems against another, but realizing that we all have struggles, and that we are blessed beyond compare to just live, breathe, and experience this magical gift called life. There are builders and destroyers in this world, and you can choose which one you will be. Will you neglect your responsibility and forfeit your own happiness in the process? Or will you build a better world?

DOUBLE THE PAYOFF

As we are created to create, we are most fulfilled when we facilitate positive change and build toward a better future. You will be surprised the impact you can have simply by adopting an attitude of service and cultivating a spirit of generosity. At times, it's tempting to believe our small acts or incidental kindness are inconsequential, but the reality is that even the smallest gesture can send positive effects rippling through countless lives.

Our goal should not be to measure or quantify what we give as much as it is to practice giving as a part of who we are. When each of us does our part to care for others, we inevitably improve life for all of us. We pay it forward and double the payoff, blessed both in the present and in the future.

Like any contract, there's something given, and something taken. As you recognize that you have a social responsibility to make a positive impact, you are committing to giving of your time, talent, or treasure to a particular cause, idea, or need. In return, you will get the benefit of serving another in love, of having more meaning and purpose in your life, and knowing that your life transcends meeting your own personal needs.

I'm often amazed at how many people want to make a donation or endow a charity as a once-in-a-lifetime event. Certainly, these contributions may be in the millions and produce change that continues on for decades. When I hear about such large one-time gifts, however, my take-away is to also practice giving each day. Clearly, I'm not trying to match donations or compete, but I also don't want to wait until I reach a certain dollar amount before blessing others, given the ever-present, immediate needs around us daily.

I suspect there's a reason that many ultra-wealthy individuals end up naming hospital wings, university buildings, and foundations after themselves: They're looking to achieve a type of immortality by trying to show that their lives and wealth had the meaning and purpose of helping others. This kind of charitable giving is wonderful, but it should not inhibit the rest of us from doing what we can today. Though most of us are not in a position or even have the desire to have things named after us, we can still make a positive impact by serving another in love, whether at a small or larger level.

The goal is not to attract attention or showcase our generosity. Something small to you could be something momentous to another person. Even offering a kind word or taking the time to spend with another could have an incredible positive impact that you may not get to know about. In your heart, of course, you can always celebrate knowing when you've shared yourself and your resources. You can know that you did something good, which is its own reward.

On the other hand, during those occasions when others might see you give, it can also be a positive example and inspire them to give as well. The generous gift of one individual can become a spark that ignites an entire community of people to give and to serve those in need. But trying to be noticed or setting yourself up as an example usually undermines the power of your generosity. Eventually, people realize that your focus is not on serving others but on generating attention for yourself and what others think of you.

BURDEN OR BLESSING

The Bible states that the best prayers and most generous acts of service are the ones that others don't even know about (Matthew 6:3). These are the ones that you did without revealing to the community at large for acknowledgement. Sometimes the recipient doesn't even know where your gift came from! Even when others don't know that you served them in some way, you still know in your heart that you did the right thing. Serve and love for the sole purpose of doing the right thing, and in time, you will realize the rewards of your actions in ways that you may have never dreamed could come true.

This hidden impact reminds me of a song that we sang years ago in church. The song is about a person that gets to heaven, unsure if they had any positive impact in this life. As they enter the pearly gates, they see a long line of people: the child they taught at Sunday School, a neighbor with whom they shared meals, a family member they cared for, and a friend they encouraged. Because of this individual's lifelong generosity, the people in this long line enjoyed more positive lives, and then in turn, served others accordingly.

You likely have no idea how long the line of people will be that you have helped—and the good news is that you still have time to serve even more. Until you pass from this planet, you can always share whatever you have—a smile, a compliment, a meal, a paycheck. Just remember that as you continue to love and serve, you receive more joy than if you hoard life's treasure for yourself.

No one gets to take one single dollar with them when they die. No matter how many houses, boats, cars, designer clothes, and status symbols you own, they mean nothing unless you share them and use them to improve the lives of others. Whether it's another person, cause, community, or environmental issue, I encourage you to recognize how you can be a positive force for good.

Your social contract is not a burden but a blessing!

CHAPTER 11

MAKE YOUR MONEY ON THE BUY

"Strategy is a commodity, execution is an art."

--PETER DRUCKER

I once spoke with investors from a large German firm who told me they had to buy $1 *billion* properties and larger to have them even show up in a "meaningful way" on their balance sheet. This requisite motivated them only to focus on enormous and expensive office buildings in places like New York City, Boston, Miami, and Chicago. Undeterred by their target acquisitions, I encouraged them to invest in a larger industrial warehouse portfolio that Northstar planned to acquire, an investment that could make much higher returns and provide more diversification than one trophy skyscraper in Manhattan.

These investors stated that such an investment as I was offering, while potentially lucrative, simply didn't fit their business model. They would have to buy a tremendous number of industrial properties just to equal the size of one trophy office building purchase. Consequently, Northstar's offering did not make sense for them to pursue since logistically, at least as they saw it, they could pour their money into one unique property more easily and efficiently. Their struggle, they explained as if I hadn't grasped their rationale, emerged from the very limited number of mega-priced landmark properties.

We parted on amicable, professional terms, but I couldn't help but wonder about the wisdom in their business model.

BRAGGING RIGHTS

Indeed, everyone has their own problems in life, from billionaires to those with very little in the bank, complete with different motivations and corporate goals than just making a solid return on an investment. Real estate investors often get caught up in their own egos when buying assets. They get emotionally attached to specific addresses, cities, glass towers, well-known structures, landmark buildings and other such assets, seemingly forgetting that the main purpose of investing capital is to make a profit.

I've seen this status-driven motivation emerge especially with foreign investors, similar to the German company that came into the U.S. market looking for prestigious investment opportunities that will instantly put them on the radar as international giants. They are attracted to trophy properties in well-known gateway cities, such as New York, Boston, Los Angeles, San Francisco, and Miami, and end up overpaying to buy an asset, just so they can boast about owning an exclusive property in such a major market. Some even like to brag about how they outspent the market with the high price they paid, as if such a feat not only fulfilled their business model but should command envy and admiration. Sometimes, these groups have so much capital to spend within each quarter or fiscal year that they need to buy trophy properties just to meet their expenditure goals.

In my business model, however, this approach "throws the baby out with the bathwater," as my parents used to say. These investors seem to have lost sight of the primary reason to invest in real estate: *profitability*. While there are many ways to make money in real estate, one of the best is to "make money on the buy." This strategy means that you should try to acquire properties at the best value, relative to the current market values and their replacement-cost values. This approach sets limits on the investor's purchases in order to avoid the very trap so many others seem to fall into—overpaying because of emotion, status, and bragging rights.

HIGHER THAN AVERAGE

When I founded Northstar Commercial Partners in 2000, I focused on buying attractive commercial real estate assets that could generate a 25% or higher Internal Rate of Return (known as an IRR), a variable based on the average yearly return on the invested dollars, taking into account duration of time, and when distributions were paid. To this day, we still focus on the same types of opportunities, and have continued to do so, whether the economy is strong, depressed, or somewhere in between. While a 25% annualized return is a very high return on equity invested, especially for foreign investors who are used to single digit annual returns, I have always believed that if you're investing in real estate, you should generate higher-than-average returns, relative to a given property's risk profile, size, expertise required for renovation, and other costs.

Though my company's average return over several decades has been higher than this goal, it remains our targeted return for opportunistic investments even now that we've grown dramatically. Over the years and through hundreds of deals, I have proven that you can make such returns not only in the strong markets where a lot of people make money, but also in the worst economies. In fact, we have made some of our highest returns when the economy was in very poor condition! While there are always variables beyond anyone's control, I'm convinced this rate of success is not due to luck but results from our investment philosophy.

REVERSE THE RISK

As part of "making money on the buy" at Northstar, I decided to focus on acquiring vacant or distressed properties. When an asset is leased up, most buyers can evaluate the income stream in place from the tenants, apply a cap rate, and thus determine the value. Though the price may fluctuate a little, these assets are openly marketed, exposed to the largest prospective buyer pool, and negotiated competitively. But these properties offer very little margin for making a profit. That's why, as I explained in Chapter 8, I focus on finding diamonds in the rough—because they present the best opportunities for making money on the buy.

By focusing on acquiring vacant properties, there is a lot less demand. Many buyers, including public Real Estate Investment Trusts (REITS), and institutional investors, are searching for cash-flowing properties that will help support their stock price, investor distributions, and high-operating expenses. These groups typically believe that it's less risky to buy a fully leased cash-flowing asset, but I'm convinced it may actually be *more* risky than buying a completely vacant property!

In the leased-asset scenario, the income stream identified when they underwrote the property and which they rely on can vanish if their tenant(s) suddenly vacate the property or go bankrupt. The investor is then left holding the bag on a high-priced property with no income. Depending on the price paid for the building, they may be forced to raise lease rates higher than current market rates, or they may incur further costs to re-lease the property such as tenant improvement dollars, lease commissions, holding costs, and so on. These costs only further inflate their cost basis in the property, making their potential returns even lower, if they make returns at all.

On the other hand, buying a vacant property that seems more risky on the outset since there is no income in place can ultimately minimize the actual risk. Because it's vacant, we can quickly determine the value, whereas you need to underwrite each tenant in a leased building scenario, including the probability of them staying or leaving, the costs of operational expenses, and other potential tenant-reliant variables. With a vacant property, you only need to underwrite the purchase price, plus the cost of improvements and holding period, along with securing new tenants. Thus, the underwriting process for these properties with unfulfilled potential is much simpler.

As there are fewer buyers for a vacant property, we can buy them at more attractive prices relative to the market. At Northstar Commercial Partners, we try to acquire the vacant assets at 50% or less of their replacement cost value. This means that if a property would cost

$70 million to replicate, we want to buy it for $35 million or less. You may question why a seller would agree to such a discount, and there are many reasons. These often include financial distress for the owner, their inability to fund the improvements and lease costs required, or their need to own cash-flowing assets only.

SEE PAST THE PINK

We have proven that there are always deals in the marketplace, if you're willing to be creative, flexible, and can execute promptly. As we now own assets in 17 states throughout the U.S., we have seen and participated in a wide spectrum of deals. This experience gives us a larger track record, and greater ability to execute on transactions, based on what we've learned and seen others attempt. Whereas a lot of companies talk about buying value and executing on deals, we actually do it. Our preference is to buy vacant assets, as we can underwrite them promptly, acquire them quickly, and improve those assets immediately upon purchase.

This latter point, renovating and improving the purchased property as quickly as possible, is key. You must be able to reposition the properties and "remove the hair" that would delay tenants or buyers from occupancy. Such transformations are not easy or instantaneous, as it often takes years of experience to decide what improvements should be made to a building. These upgrades may include new carpet, paint, higher clear-height doors, demolition of inadequate or dysfunctional space, remediation of an environmental issue, just to name a few.

Many investors are afraid of making these renovation decisions and changes, as they worry that they're making the wrong choices.

Instead, they decide to wait to see what a tenant or buyer wants, and then try to tailor improvements to their prospective occupants' desires. But this is the worst strategy of all! Most tenants or buyers cannot envision a completed space, in terms of what it can look like cleaned up, repositioned, and improved. All they can see is the vacant dilapidated space in front of them with all of its blemishes, problems, and limitations. A good investor must help them see the finished product.

I learned this lesson during the summer after graduating from CU Boulder, and working at my father's Century 21 residential real estate office in Upstate New York. I had shown a couple from the city a cute vacation home several times. They absolutely loved the house, but the wife could not get past the outdated, '70's pink countertops throughout the home. Although I told her several times that these could be easily removed and quickly replaced with her selection, she could not see past the pink! Consequently, this sale did not go through. But the experience made a lasting impression, and to this day, I focus on doing the work for prospective tenants or buyers prior to their viewing. By removing the hair and providing a fresh, contemporary look, I do everything possible to create the vision for our potential tenant/buyer.

OUT OF THE CHUTE

Through the process of making your money on the buy, you don't have to make-up for a poor investment. When your cost basis is too high, you're then forever trying to cut expenses, increase income, and enhance efficiencies, all in order to make up for the high cost basis. In such situations, it becomes a matter of breaking even rather than making a significant profit. By buying right, however, you have already made money coming out of the chutes, which gives you a distinct advantage right away.

In western rodeos, bronco busting and bull riding events use chutes to contain the rider on the animal until the gate opens and the clock begins ticking to see how long they can last in the saddle. Those first steps out of the chute are crucial to a good ride and helps determine the score the judges give for that rider's performance. By paying beneath a property's market value, especially its potential value after improvements, you're ahead of the game and starting "out of the chute" on good footing. Adding upgrades and making renovations only increases the income and profit from that property.

Turning a greater-than-average profit also provides stronger cash flow for your other asset purchases and future property improvement costs. This strategy also affords you the opportunity to cut more competitive deals than your competition, be more patient for the right deal, and be more creative in the use of the space, as your cost basis is much lower, allowing you to make better choices that yield a higher potential return.

One of my very wise private investors who owns a very famous residential development company, once told me, "Brian, what can take you a moment to buy, can take you a lifetime to sell." Though he told me this almost twenty years ago, I remember it well to this day. If you buy the wrong asset at the wrong price, it may take you decades to try to create value and finally sell it. If you buy a mediocre asset at the right price, however, good things can happen for you.

Each real estate investment is like setting sail with a ship from a safe harbor. If the price is too high, and you're sailing in the wrong direction even by the slightest of degrees, then you will end up in an entirely different port than your original destination. You can eliminate many of the variables, both known and unknown, but staying on course with the right strategy. If you're willing to be patient, choose wisely, and hold fast to making your money on the buy, then your successful voyage can last a lifetime!

CHAPTER 12

RELATIONSHIPS. RELATIONSHIPS. RELATIONSHIPS!

"I believe that you can get everything in life you want if you will just help enough other people get what they want."

--ZIG ZIGLAR

You see it on billboards, yard signs, business cards, and online pop-up banners: *"Location, location, location!"* In real estate, whether residential or commercial, this timeless adage proves itself over and over again. While I agree that location plays a central, integral role in the value of a property, when it comes to building a successful real estate business, there's another just as important ingredient: *relationships*.

In business as in life, who you know matters just as much as what you know. And if you're investing in real estate, your success relies not only on attracting tenants and buyers for your properties but also on connecting with sellers, builders, contractors, renovators, designers, neighbors, other investors, along with government and community leaders. Depending on the scale and scope of your business, you will most likely need to interact with international clients and investors as well. In these situations, you often discover that human connection transcends any language barriers or cultural differences. No matter how important a property's location may be, your success ultimately comes from your relationships.

LEGACY OF DREAMS

As I've shared, I did not grow up in a family of influence and wealth. None of us graduated from Ivy League schools, came from a political dynasty, or mingled with wealthy socialites. My ancestors were hard working, humble people who left a legacy of strength, self-sufficiency, and sacrifice to subsequent generations. My grandparents were immigrants, in search of freedom to achieve their American Dream through perseverance and hard work. My parents were first-generation Americans without college educations who nonetheless succeeded as entrepreneurs, providing better lives for their children than they had experienced.

My three sisters, one brother, and I inherited this strong work ethic, and it shows in how we've each pursued our various dreams. Among the five of us, three have graduated from college, and two of us have started our own companies. We embody the essence of the dreams of our ancestors. From immigrants to entrepreneurs, our great nation was forged on the anvil of dedication, perseverance, and resilience. This same process continues to shape our country today, a key part of what makes our United States so appealing to individuals and families around the world.

In addition to the incredible work ethic I learned from my parents and grandparents, I also learned the value of relationships. They taught me how to get along with others to achieve shared goals, how to resolve conflicts and still maintain the relationships, how to build rapport and bond with other like-minded entrepreneurs. Human beings are fundamentally social, and we need each other. Nowhere is this more apparent than in business, particularly in commercial real estate. If you're serious about realizing your dreams, then relationships are your building blocks.

LISTEN AND LEARN

The art of relationships is really rather simple: listen and engage. Of course, getting to know people and building a history of interactions over time can often become quite complicated and nuanced. Nonetheless, you would be surprised what you can learn from others simply by listening. Our lives are cluttered with sound bites and scripts based on the roles we play each day. When you really slow down and listen to others, it's amazing what they're willing to share with you. Once you've established authentic relationships with successful individuals, you often discover their willingness to help you.

So many times, people will try to tell you what they know or what you need to close a deal if you will simply listen. Some of the best wisdom I've ever received came as the result of my asking, "How did you do it? How did you find a solution?" Similarly, I will often ask others, "What did you learn? What would you do if you were in my shoes?" Asking these kinds of questions requires humility but also signals respect. Even competitors and individuals with very different viewpoints will gladly share their wisdom with you if they sense you respect them.

In your pursuit of learning from others, don't limit yourself only to the apparent power brokers—the CEOs, wealthy investors, and experts. Rather, it is better to meet and learn from people of all walks of life, to ascertain how their life lessons can apply to what you are going through or are trying to achieve. While it's important to cultivate relationships with key players, you can learn so much from players behind the scenes. These people may not even be in your field of work or business. Whether it be a taxi cab driver, janitor, office assistant, CEO, or a head of state, you can learn something valuable from each person.

When you're willing to engage with others on a human level, you look beyond their appearance, title, and role and respect them as another unique individual with enormous life expertise. Sometimes the janitor knows much more about the specific details of a property than its owner. An investor's assistant may exert as much influence as the board of directors. A hard-working contractor may lack degrees in engineering but know more about load-bearing beams than the highly credentialed architect drawing up the blueprint for a remodel.

MORE SIMILAR THAN DIFFERENT

As you seek out different and varying connections, you can make links to what you hope to achieve, in ways that may have never been done before. You can also learn from those who have "been there and done that." Most people want to share their expertise and feel valued for their life experience. When you look beyond someone's appearance, job title, or current role, you will receive wisdom from surprising sources.

My advice for connecting with others may seem obvious, yet I often see others fail to practice it regularly. It's simple but incredibly effective: key on the similarities among people rather than the differences. Every human being wants to feel appreciated, needs encouragement, and enjoys acceptance. You would be surprised how sharing a meal, talking about children or other family members, and discussing common interests like sports can help you connect. Don't stick to a script or force conversations but do try to engage with others in ways that are natural and authentic.

While you will inevitably make your own mistakes in the process of becoming an entrepreneur, those unexpected problems, failed deals, and troublesome properties are often the best teachers for future success. When you experience conflict with stakeholders in a deal, it's important to learn all you can through the process. Don't dismiss individuals just because they don't agree with you or see your point of view. It can be incredibly disarming when others realize we're trying to understand them even if we still disagree with them.

Don't assume you know their motivations or ambitions. Especially with aggressive competitors, stubborn property sellers, and finicky tenants, you want to practice diplomacy. Try to balance your own interests with a more objective perspective that allows you to see the proverbial win-win solutions. Compromise is not a sign of weakness but a tool for negotiation. With each awkward discussion or prickly conversation, you learn to communicate more effectively. Obviously, at the end of the day, you are in business to make a profit—not to befriend others or donate to charity. But the best business is built on real relationships.

EXPONENTIAL GROWTH

Through quality authentic relationships, you can also grow your business and generate new solutions in exponential ways, faster. Through meeting people and learning from them, you will build friendships with these people in time. You will gain a sense of who they are and what's important to them. As friends like to help friends, they will in turn introduce you to new business opportunities, innovative ideas, and other dynamic contacts. People like to do business with people they know and trust, and this feeling only grows with the more people you meet.

Please note, though, that these relationships need to be real, authentic, and true. You can't fake it until you make it when it comes to caring about people. Others had rather you remain reserved and professional rather than pretend to be interested in them when you're not. And most of the time, they can tell when you're just being polite or being overly friendly just to get what you want from them. If you think about it, can't you usually tell when someone is genuine versus just going through the motions? And do you tend to trust those people who seem slick and solicitous?

Instead, treat others like you want to be treated. The Golden Rule is universal across every culture I've ever encountered. There is simply no substitute for showing respect, kindness, and authentic engagement with others. If you want to enrich your life personally and grow your business professionally, then be genuine. Be deliberate about investing in others' lives and building friendships. Serve others by being the friend you wish you had. When you practice this kind of caring service over time, meaningful relationships and enduring friendships will inevitably blossom.

PEOPLE OVER PROFIT

Your relational reputation is your greatest asset. At Northstar Commercial Partners, we're motivated by a mindset of opportunity not only for our investors but all stakeholders with whom we interact. We put people over profit on our properties. There are plenty of deals and real estate assets to acquire, but we only want to do the best deals, ones that will make a profit for us and our capital investors. Naturally, this mission reinforces the importance we put on relationships. We're always driven by relationships in the pursuit of building friendships and serving stakeholders. Relationships and friendships come first, and we do not risk jeopardizing them just to increase profit or get ahead of our competitors. We're committed to remaining honest, true, focused, and loyal, trusting that good things will come to us in the long run, as well as the short run, if we put people first.

As the bullets are flying in the trenches of life, we remain alongside our partners, knowing we are stronger on the field of battle together. Such commitment also makes our partners more committed to us, as they realize we can accomplish more together. Yes, there are ups and downs in life and in investments, and sometimes others will seek to betray you or exploit your dedication to integrity. But being the friend you wish you had as well as the investment partner you can always count on is more than worth it. In the long run, you will not only succeed in business but will enhance your life with a garden of cherished friends.

THE "I'S" HAVE IT

In establishing and cultivating relationships, I've discovered that being proactive and initiating shared activities facilitates opportunities for growth. I like practicing what I now call the "Three I's": initiate, invite, include. Whether it be hosting our annual investors' retreat at a dude ranch in the Rocky Mountains of Colorado each year, cheering on the Broncos or CU football team with guests in our corporate suites, taking prospective partners on day trips to ski in the high country, or volunteering time and money to philanthropic causes, our Northstar team and I regularly practice cultivating relationships.

This practice extends beyond Northstar and is just part of my DNA. As I travel throughout the U.S. each year, and as I visit various cities and parts of the country, I always ask friends and colleagues who I should meet in these areas. Though many of these meetings are not business related or do not turn into immediate deals, I try to learn something unique or new from each new person I encounter. We may have different backgrounds and business pursuits, but they often teach me something about their area, the local market, or the prevailing attitudes of residents. They often tell me which local restaurant has the best rib eye or which landmarks are not to be missed. They remind me why I love meeting new people so much!

RISK TO REAP REWARDS

Relationships wield incredible power to determine the success of your business for two fundamental reasons: they reveal what you want to emulate and what you want to avoid. Listen and learn from each person you meet, and figure out if there are elements you would like to incorporate into your own life, to remove, or to avoid altogether. As humans, we are designed to be relational, and to grow in relationships with others. We should take this innate social hardwiring and use it as a lifeline to learn, grow, and thrive.

I'm convinced that most people ultimately want to help other people. Though some may seem busy, standoffish, or even mean at times, part of them also wants to help others and contribute to their success. Relationships have helped to grow my business, to develop my abilities as an entrepreneur and business owner, and to increase my knowledge base on a variety of subjects. More importantly, they enrich my life and make me a better person.

Relationships help us to grow better, smarter, and faster. In fact, this principle has become a mantra at my company, a vital part of our unique culture. Daily, we ask ourselves how we can become "better, smarter, and faster" in our work life, business execution, and personal vision? If you ask this question regularly, and truly listen to your subconscious mind, you will be surprised how new ideas that will support these three objectives will come forth. Don't be afraid to ask the question and be sure to act upon the answers. Take risks in your relationships in order to reap their rewards.

If you want to enhance your life in every area, then make every effort to build your relationships in more deliberate, meaningful, and focused ways. Even if you are an introvert by nature and relationships force you out of your comfort zone, you will discover it's well worth the risk. Build upon your existing relationships and make a positive effort to begin new ones as well. You will be surprised how these will grow exponentially over time, if you just put yourself out there.

Your life—and your business—will be all the better for it!

CHAPTER 13

GOAL TENDING

"The thing about goals is that living without them is a lot more fun, in the short run. It seems to me, though, that the people who get things done, who lead, who grow and who make an impact...those people have goals."

--SETH GODIN

In sports, goaltending is the defensive prevention of an opponent's scoring attempt. In soccer and hockey, the position of goaltender is key to the success of the game, requiring someone with lightning-fast reflexes and amazing agility. When playing basketball, however, goaltending is a violation because it's perceived as interfering with the natural consequence after an opponent has shot the ball.

While I appreciate the importance of playing defensively, the kind of goal tending (two words, not one) I advocate is much more proactive. Because my goal tending relies on establishing, nurturing, and shepherding your goals. Goal setting and goal management must be part of your lifestyle, both personally and professionally, if you want to succeed. It's okay to act instinctively or fly by the seat of your pants occasionally, but this will not produce consistent results over time. Tending your goals allows you to set them and adjust them as new information emerges, conditions change, or circumstances vary. Goal tending will help you win the game of life!

TARGET PRACTICE

There is nothing quite like setting goals and then actually accomplishing them through planning, persistence, and perseverance. As humans, we were designed to create and achieve—it's part of our DNA. Whether we're planting a garden, landscaping our yard, cooking a meal, writing a novel, painting a portrait, or launching a startup, we each have the ability to enjoy bringing order from chaos. Such actions help to give us a sense of meaning, purpose, and accomplishment. Many variables in our life remain beyond our control, but doesn't it make sense to influence outcomes as much as possible?

You'd be surprised how many people ask me for advice, counsel, or recommendations on a major decision or potential business deal—*without having a clear goal in mind!* Without a mission and goals to support its fulfillment, an entrepreneur becomes a victim of circumstance, forced to rely on whim, chance, or a lucky break. They might tread water for a while or ride in the wake of a booming economy. But eventually, they will begin to sink without long-term planning and goal tending.

Entrepreneurs, however, who dream big, set specific goals, and follow through on them, almost always succeed. They know their organization's mission and how to achieve it and then sustain it as they grow. They understand the vital importance of writing goals down and breaking them into strategic action points that contribute in some way toward that goal's fulfillment. They aren't afraid to drop certain goals, revise others, and generate new ones in order to achieve their desired results.

I'm convinced that if you look at the work and lifestyle habits of any successful person in any field, you will find a common denominator in their goals. I'm not only talking about success in business or earning profits but about their enjoyment and satisfaction with life. Lately I've noticed so many popular self-improvement books on how to be happy. While I've not read them all, the few I've picked up stress the importance of identifying what you find fulfilling in life and then setting goals in its pursuit. You'll never hit the bull's eye if you don't have a target!

GET IT IN WRITING

Every January 1st, I sit down to write out my goals for the entire year. Studies show that you are more likely to achieve your goals, if you actually write them down. When you commit them to writing, you're also more inclined to review them periodically not only to remind yourself but also to evaluate your progress. As the years have passed, I have started selecting the number of my goals based on the new year. This means for 2018 I selected 18 goals, and for 2019, I chose 19. As the years progress, I may need to dial back and simply focus on 7-10 goals, which are probably more manageable and achievable, but for the time being, I like my current system.

My goals are written in my journal. I started journaling when I was in high school, and I've kept this habit ever since. With quite a few completed journals on my shelf, I consider each one a treasure chest of ideas, memories, and lessons learned. As I read through them from time-to-time, I can see what I was thinking about during a particular time or past season. These reviews provide wonderful insight and allow me to see progress made and goals achieved. Often I notice patterns in past events that were not visible at the time when I first wrote about them. I've also discovered that past worries can become catalysts for my greatest achievements. Looking back, I've learned to appreciate the many special moments and extraordinary experiences with which I've been blessed in my life.

When I journal, I write anything and everything that's on my mind or in my heart. I'll write about topics, concepts, an interesting movie I watched, life changes, or a lead on a prospective property. It's good to explore and expound upon these ideas in written form, and I have found it helpful to developing my thought process. Writing forces me to slow down and think through what I understand about a situation or issue.

As for my goals, I simply write them down, often bulleting them in a list. They range from personal development, like learning to speak Spanish more fluently, to business, such as hitting a certain financial goal, to family, perhaps planning a vacation for all of us. I've found it's helpful to include specifics that can be measured, within a finite time frame. So instead of writing down, "I hope to be a better person this year," I might jot down, "I hope to be a better person this year by spending at least one day per week serving at the local homeless shelter as well as spending at least ten hours of focused quality time with my kids, without looking at my phone during any of those times." Then as I volunteer, I'll go back to provide an update, or after spending time with my kids, I'll describe what we did or talked about.

Writing out your goals gives you perspective and allows you to consider them from different points of view. Sometimes I'll discover that I've set a goal that's presently too complicated or requires more time than I can currently invest. Instead of scrapping the goal entirely, however, I usually break it down into bite-sized pieces. For instance, if I don't have time to study and really learn more Spanish this year, instead I can commit to listening to audio instructions for conversational Spanish when I'm on the road or learn the ten most common verbs and all their forms. Any progress toward your goal is better than no progress. Over time, each small achievement contributes toward the larger goal you're building.

BHAGS

As part of your goals, I encourage you to choose "Big Hairy Audacious Goals," or BHAGS for short. These are outrageous and audacious goals that truly challenge you to new heights. These might be targets like "double my income from the previous year," or "compete in an Iron Man by year's end." They should be goals that seem impossible based on where you are at present.

But creating some BHAGS for yourself can generate surprising results. If you set such large goals and are truly committed to achieving them, you will be surprised how your mind will work daily to achieve them. And even if you don't reach them within your time frame, you can revise them on your next list knowing you're that much closer. Don't be afraid of pushing yourself to new heights and chasing after crazy challenges. BHAGS will make your blood flow, invigorate your imagination as you seek resourceful ways to make them happen, and provide you with targets bigger than your current goals.

In addition to my yearly goals and BHAGS, I also write down the tasks I want to complete on a daily, weekly, or monthly basis. I usually write these shorter-term goals on a yellow legal pad of paper, which I keep in my business binder and review daily. In addition to writing down the action item, I'll often place the initials or name of the person who I've assigned to tackle that point. This allows me to follow up with them, and when I meet with my staff, I can quickly look at the list and ask them for an update on their progress for that particular item.

One of the best things about writing down my other short term goals and tasks is that when they're accomplished, I can run a line through them. Seeing items completed helps me account for my time and energy, knowing where I've invested it. You would be surprised how satisfying this exercise can be! I believe seeing what you've actually been able to knock off your list is very empowering for the subconscious mind. As you cross off these items, you may feel inspired to tackle more items on your list. You may enjoy an adrenaline rush that fuels your ability to get more done than you planned or expected. Though I've never cleared off my entire list, it's good to see them reduced from 3-5 pages to 1-2 pages.

SAILING TO ITHACA

Goal tending is vital. If you don't have short, medium, and long-term goals, you end up sailing like a ship without a destination. Adrift on the ocean tides, you're tossed about and forced to ride the waves without knowing where you're going or where you'll end up. Instead, you must chart a course for the port where you want to arrive.

You must consider the life you wish to live in the long term, and allow the short-term goals to fulfill the medium-term ones, which will then contribute to progress for the long-term goals. Don't be afraid to "shoot for the moon" in designing the most amazing life that you can dream. Even if you come up short, the journey will be rich and rewarding, and you will have achieved and experienced more than if you lived a life with no goals or purpose at all.

I often rely on quotations, poems, and biographies of great leaders to inspire my goal tending. One of my all-time favorite sources of inspiration is the poem "Ithaca." I found this while in college and have kept a printed and framed copy near me ever since. The poem is about setting sail for an epic voyage to fulfill your goal of reaching this magical, wonderful place called Ithaca. It's about enjoying your journey along the way and realizing that your journey is just as important as your destination. Even if you never reach your Ithaca, as events may change your course along the way, the pursuit of Ithaca will still give you the journey, which is wonderful, beautiful, and worthwhile in itself.

ITHACA

When you set out for Ithaca
ask that your way be long,
full of adventure, full of instruction.
The Laistrygonians and the Cyclops,
angry Poseidon—do not fear them:
such as these you will never find
as long as your thought is lofty, as long as a rare
emotion touch your spirit and your body.
The Laistrygonians and the Cyclops,
angry Poseidon - you will not meet them
unless you carry them in your soul,
unless your soul raise them up before you.

Ask that your way be long.
At many a Summer dawn to enter
with what gratitude, what joy -
ports seen for the first time;
to stop at Phoenician trading centres,
and to buy good merchandise,
mother of pearl and coral, amber and ebony,
and sensuous perfumes of every kind,
sensuous perfumes as lavishly as you can;
to visit many Egyptian cities,
to gather stores of knowledge from the learned.

Have Ithaca always in your mind.
Your arrival there is what you are destined for.
But don't in the least hurry the journey.
Better it last for years,
so that when you reach the island you are old,
rich with all you have gained on the way,
not expecting Ithaca to give you wealth.
Ithaka gave you a splendid journey.
Without her you would not have set out.
She hasn't anything else to give you.

And if you find her poor, Ithaca hasn't deceived you.
So wise you have become, of such experience,
that already you'll have understood what these Ithacas mean.

Constantine P. Cavafy, 1911

As you set your goals and sails for the future, I encourage you to focus upon your "Ithaca."

IN THE ARENA

As you create your goals and set sail for the future, I encourage you to focus upon your very own Ithaca. Every day is an opportunity to make one change, one improvement, and one accomplishment that moves you closer to fulfilling one of your goals. Some days you will make progress in inches, and some days in yards, and some days you will reach the shore of Ithaca or another destination. The goal is to continuously try, knowing there may be storms, delays, and other obstacles along the way. Whether you achieve the final goal or reach Ithaca, at least you tried. Engaging in a whole-hearted attempt to achieve your goals is better than most people will ever do.

Goals require you to risk, day after day, again and again. When I've been disappointed or fallen short of my goal, I find renewed inspiration in another great passage that I keep framed in my office. It's from a speech by U.S. President Teddy Roosevelt, who himself overcame astounding setbacks and tragedies to enjoy a remarkable life of service to others. He reminds us all to avoid playing it safe, to set BHAGS and go after them, to get up when we fall down. He encourages us to make goal tending an inherent part of who we are.

"It is not the critic who counts; not the man who points out how the strong man stumbles, or where the doer of deeds could have done them better. The credit belongs to the man who is actually in the arena, whose face is marred by dust and sweat and blood; who strives valiantly; who errs, who comes short again and again, because there is no effort without error and shortcoming; but who does actually strive to do the deeds; who knows great enthusiasms, the great devotions; who spends himself in a worthy cause; who at the best knows in the end the triumph of high achievement, and who at the worst, if he fails, at least fails while daring greatly, so that his place shall never be with those cold and timid souls who neither know victory nor defeat."

Theodore Roosevelt, from the speech
"Citizenship in a Republic," 1910

CHAPTER 14

BUILDING YOUR LEGACY

*"Success means using your knowledge
and experience to satisfy yourself.
Significance means using your
knowledge and experience to change
the lives of others."*

--BOB BUFORD

As a history buff and seasoned traveler, I love combining the two passions by visiting sites where history was made. There's just something magical about walking through Mount Vernon, George Washington's Virginia home on the banks of the Potomac River, and knowing that I'm standing on the same wooden floors where our nation's great first president once stood. I get the same feeling touring Thomas Jefferson's Monticello or seeing Independence Hall in Philadelphia. The past feels so alive in these remarkable structures that I can just imagine what it must have been like over 200 years ago when our country was founded.

My love for history is not limited to just my beloved United States. I've been blessed to see some of the world's most iconic, historic locations, sites where battles determined the fate of millions, where writers like Shakespeare honed their craft, where religions were born and royalty crowned. My connection to these places is usually not as strong as the ones I visit in my homeland. Nonetheless, I've marveled at the amazing architecture of ancient pyramids in the Egyptian desert as well as the Sydney Opera House in Australia. I've been just as moved by the sacred temples of Angkor Wat as I have been when staring up at the ceiling of the Sistine Chapel to see Michelangelo's renowned mural.

Visiting these landmarks and famous locations always ignites my imagination. As I imagine the events, conversations, and history-making moments that transpired there, I can't help but wonder about the individual lives of the men and women whose stories are intertwined with these great places. How did our Founding Fathers resolve their differences when establishing a government for this new nation? What was it to see Shakespeare's plays when they were first performed at the Globe Theater? How did Michelangelo manage his backaches from painting on the ceiling for so long?

When I was younger, I was often impressed by the way historic sites immortalized the stories of the many people passing through their doors. But the older I get, the more I realize that while these places are often associated with certain people, they are only places. The reason we're touched by the lives of people we never met is because of the legacy they left in their actions and character. As much as I love the Lincoln Memorial in Washington, D.C., the magnificent stone sculpture is not what keeps the legacy of the Great Emancipator alive. His words, his actions, his anguished decisions remain the building blocks for his enduring legacy that time can never erase.

No matter how special a place might be, no matter how magnificent a palace might appear, they're still just buildings. No monument can ever replace the true legacy of a life well lived. A lasting legacy is built not with bricks and mortar but with service and sacrifice. Legacy is the kind of life you built not the building you left behind.

HISTORICAL OR HISTORIC

Visiting so many different places around the world, I've learned an important distinction. It's a lesson my high school English teacher first taught me, but it didn't mean much at the time. Only by traveling the globe and seeing sites and settings that transcend cultural, social, and historical boundaries have I learned the real difference between two closely related words: "historical" and "historic."

The difference is actually quite simple. Calling something "historical" just means that it's old! Like the terms "antique" and "vintage," how old is often relative. Generally, something labeled historical, particularly a home or building, must be at least fifty years old. In order to be registered with the local historical society, many structures must be at least one hundreds years old. Regardless of the minimum, the historical distinction relies on quantity of time passed.

Describing something as "historic," on the other hand, means that it's not only historical but also significant, famous, memorable, or extraordinary. Historic places stand out because history was made there. Many houses might be deemed historical because of their age, but only a few are truly historic—perhaps because of the architect who designed it (like Frank Lloyd Wright), the person who grew up there (like President Lincoln), the celebrity who made it famous (as Elvis did with Graceland), or an event that happened there (a stop on the Underground Railroad).

But even historic buildings, homes, and landmarks don't last forever. They're subject to damage from natural disasters like tornadoes and hurricanes as well as destructive forces like fire, as we've seen in recent years with Notre Dame and Windsor Castle. Even if they manage to remain secure from storms, fires, earthquakes, and mudslides, they will deteriorate and crumble unless managed and renovated on a regular basis.

In fact, if there's one thing you learn in real estate and construction, it's that no building lasts forever. Many times it's more cost effective to demolish an old building instead of restoring it. People often buy properties for the location only to scrape the existing structure and build one of their own. Once again, creating a legacy based on properties and possessions doesn't last.

All legacies are historical, but the ones that last are historic.

MORE THAN MATERIAL

The way to build your lasting legacy is to consider the cumulative impact of your goals. Look at the end result you want to achieve with your life and work backward from there. As you set your goals, always consider how they contribute to your legacy. When your life is all said and done, what would you like your personal legacy to be? This means not only how others will remember you as an individual but also the impact you had in their lives. What difference did your life's contribution make in the lives of others? How did you improve the condition of your home, neighborhood, community, state, country, and world?

Legacy is important to consider because it cuts through all the material stuff and goes right to the heart of what matters most. On the gravestone of most people, the person's possessions and property aren't listed but their relationships, service, and love may be cited. I've never seen "Here lies Fred, who owned a Rolex watch" or "R.I.P. Sally—She earned $1 million per year." Instead, people are remembered by whether they were a good person, if they loved their family well, and how they served their fellow human being. Whatever their legacy, if it endures you can be sure it's much more than material things. As much as leaving money to others can change their lifestyles, it only makes a difference if you invested in their lives.

Think about the kind of person you want to be when your life is over, whether that's a year from now or a hundred years from now. If you could be a witness to your personal funeral service, what do you hope people would say about you? If you knew you only had a few months to live, what would you do with your remaining time on earth? It may seem morbid or unpleasant to consider such scenarios, but they reflect the inescapable truth for all of us. Our time is limited and our days are numbered. If you don't start making them count now, they won't add up to the kind of life you ultimately want to live.

FROM SUCCESS TO SIGNIFICANCE

Looking at the legacies of others has often helped me think about my own. I suspect that's why I love history so much—not because of the valuable items or artistry found in mansions and museums but because of their links to lives in the past. I find that most of the historic places I visit are only important if they remind us of the qualities of the people they represent. The courage of a leader trying to serve their embattled country, the sacrifice of a parent for their child's future success, the generosity of an entrepreneur who believed in the power of education to change lives. Our legacy transcends any material items, money, or monuments we leave behind.

You probably won't be surprised to learn that one of my favorite books, *Halftime* by Bob Buford, focuses on legacy. This writer attained dramatic financial success at a relatively young age, but soon found himself wondering how to make his life matter. He knew there had to be more important things to do with his wealth and influence than become a competitive consumer of status trophies.

Realizing that roughly half his life was over—if he was fortunate to live the average number of years—he felt an urgency about how he lived the rest of his life. Buford explains, "Instead of facing a crisis as I approached middle age, I discovered that a new and better life lay before me. I called the process of discovery 'halftime,' and the outcome led to my second half."[1] Using this ballgame metaphor, he describes the first half of our lives as one focused on the pursuit of "success," however we may define it. The goal is to climb the career ladder, earn a certain income, and achieve a lifestyle featuring symbols, both personal and cultural, that broadcast our success.

After pursuing these during the first half of his life, Buford wanted to pause and rethink his life goals and the legacy he wanted to leave. He realized there had to be something more to life, some kind of goal that made a positive difference in other people's lives. Like a coach changing strategy in the locker room during halftime of the big game,

---

1   Bob Buford, *Halftime: Moving from Success to Significance, 20th Anniversary Edition*, (Grand Rapids, MI: Zondervan, 2015), 12.

Buford shifted focus to a different set of priorities for the final half of life's game, moving from culturally defined success to personally defined significance. "Our first half is about how to make a living, and our second half has the promise of being about how to make a life."[2]

SIMPLE GIFTS

Significance comes from loving and serving others, about making a lasting positive impact, about discovering your true purpose for being on this earth, and realizing you have only a certain amount of precious time which should not be wasted. Usually this shift occurs by realizing that after you achieve a certain level of mobility financially, then happiness comes from your relationships and shared experiences. You realize it truly is more blessed to give than to receive. You become much less concerned about what you acquire and much more focused on what you can contribute.

This is where your shift to significance informs the kind of legacy you will leave.

Legacy is about making a meaningful and lasting impact, one that is worthy to be remembered. Legacy ripples and echoes throughout the lives of those people you touched—through kindness, generosity, and compassion—down through all the generations that follow you. Investing in your legacy is not just about some grandiose achievement such as funding new campus buildings at your alma mater or creating an endowment for your favorite charity. Yes, it might include those gifts, but the real investment in your legacy comes from how you treat others every day.

---

2   Ibid, 16.

You don't have to eliminate world hunger; you simply need to nourish the hungry soul of one person's life. You don't have to set up a college scholarship fund; you merely need to share your wisdom with those seeking your counsel. You don't have to host fundraising events for thousands of people; you just have to donate your time to those you serve. Your simple gifts become significant investments in the lives of others.

It is not for us to measure the impact of our investment in another's life, but rather to see and serve their need, regardless of whether they recognize our contribution or express their gratitude. Though you can help decide what you would like your legacy to be, it will not be fully known or realized until after you are gone. Ultimately, your legacy is built by the bricks of human kindness, mutual respect, and unreserved generosity stacked on a daily basis. Over time, each building block of significance becomes the foundation for a legacy that's not merely historical but historic.

BUILD A BLESSING

Let me ask you again: If you were to pass today, what do you think people would say about your life, or *would they say anything at all?* If you're still in the first half of life and feel like you have plenty of time for significance later in life, then I caution you to remember that your days are numbered. No one knows how much time they have left on earth so you can't take your most precious commodity of time for granted.

On the other hand, if you feel like you've already passed the halfway mark in your life, you might be tempted to think it's too late to change now. But this excuse is simply not true! You can always keep the best of life ahead of you if you're willing to serve others. No matter whether you're in halftime or the fourth quarter, you can still score the drive that wins the game.

If you're satisfied with your answer, then feel free to stay the course of your life. Persevere as you continue looking for opportunities to invest your resources in service to others. But if you would hope to build a legacy of true significance that others would enjoy long after you're gone, then spend some time in reflection. Think about where and how you can make a difference and turn it into a major goal for your life. Write it down, and begin thinking and praying about what should be done to build the kind of legacy you want to leave behind.

Whatever you want your legacy to be, make it something larger than your own success. Dream beyond yourself so that you can become a catalyst for something positive, something enduring that truly benefits this planet. Build a blessing in the lives of each person you encounter today. If each of us works to leave such a legacy to bless others, the world will become a better place, one person at a time.

CHAPTER 15

THE MIRROR AND THE MIST

*"How we spend our days is, of course,
how we spend our lives."*

--ANNIE DILLARD

It's easy to think about the kind of legacy you want to leave but much more challenging to make the investments required to build it, day-in and day-out. Numerous challenges emerge to thwart your progress on a regular, if not relentless, basis. Sometimes obstacles can be removed fairly easily, but other times, you feel blindsided by a devastating loss, painful betrayal, or unexpected defeat.

These kinds of events knock the wind out of you and leave you lying on the ground, wondering when—or even if—you'll be able to stand again. Such storms often erode the life you were building and force you to start over once again or to reconsider the blueprint you've been following. Even after your circumstances have improved, the damage done to your dreams lingers on.

Like most people, I have experienced my share of setbacks and losses. The first time I realized how dramatically life can change, I was eight years old. My parents, after more than two decades of marriage, decided to divorce. Their breakup made me realize how relationships splinter over time as I watched their daily disagreements and angry attitudes turn into bitter arguments and stubborn grudges. While I knew they both loved me, I also knew I wanted to build a different kind of life than they shared.

A MIRROR DIMLY

Although my parents' divorce left my world shaken, I recovered a sense of family when my mother later remarried Bill Watson, a stone-cutter and general contractor. Our family then traded the Catskill Mountains of upstate New York for the Rockies of Colorado, moving to the Western Slope. There, Bill started his own construction company where, as I shared in previous chapters, I learned so much about the value of working hard and working smart. After a few years, Bill adopted me as his son, and we enjoyed hunting, fishing, camping, hiking, horseback riding, and building our family's home, where my mother still lives to this day.

Growing close to Bill and experiencing the joy of our happy family only made it that much more painful when he died unexpectedly. One night he returned home from meeting with a client when he suffered a severe asthma attack, collapsing on the kitchen floor in front of me before dying later that night at the hospital. At sixteen, I became the man of the house, working part-time and caring for my younger siblings while my mother returned to a local college to earn her degree. Determined to excel in school, I studied hard and led numerous extracurricular clubs and activities.

I still feel the ache of losing Bill, which was only compounded a few years ago when I lost my biological father, Bob Lambrigger. I'm blessed to have had them both in my life and their legacy lives on in me and my children. But I can't pretend to understand why Bill died so young or to deny the anger, loneliness, and grief I've endured since then.

Over the years, however, I've learned that there is simply no way to understand why. The Apostle Paul writes that in this life "we see in a mirror dimly," only knowing in part what we will one day discover in heaven (1 Corinthians 13:12, NASB). His description always reminds me of the way our bathroom mirror used to fog up from the steam of the shower, in the house where I grew up. As a teenager just learning to shave, I would get frustrated that I couldn't see my face clearly enough to bring my razor to it. I would use a towel to wipe away the steamy mist, which helped a little, but mostly I just had to wait a few minutes until the condensation lifted and my reflection returned.

So in this life we have to wait to see clearly and understand more fully why certain events happened. Instead of becoming stuck in grief, fear, or despair, I've grown in gratitude for the love and wisdom both my fathers passed on to me. Rather than remaining on the sidelines, I found the strength to build the kind of life I hope they would both be proud of.

ADVERSITY AND ADVANTAGE

I share such losses with you not for sympathy but so you can recognize the way we—all human beings—endure life's brutal storms. In fact, another one of my life's hardest seasons reminded me daily that I was not the only one suffering. During the economic downturn of 2008, Northstar struggled like thousands of other businesses at the time. I had worked my entire life to start and grow Northstar, which I had launched in 2000, into a premier commercial real estate investment company with millions of square feet of office, retail, and industrial properties across America.

But suddenly everything I had built was in jeopardy.

Banking, mortgage, and real estate markets were some of the hardest hit, and because they all tied in to our business, we struggled in the crossfire. Loans were called in from fearful lenders while other institutions closed altogether. Some tenants cancelled their leases while others simply went bankrupt and disappeared. But I wasn't about to give up without fighting with every ounce of my blood, sweat, and tears. I refused to sit back and watch my dreams go up in flames. So I worked harder than I've ever worked in my life, hustling day and night and using every penny of my personal savings to ensure Northstar would survive.

Since then, I have faced several other major disappointments and unimaginable losses. Business deals fell through. Political campaigns didn't yield the victories that I had worked so hard to secure. Important relationships unraveled. Key colleagues have passed away. But I've also enjoyed so many amazing moments and precious times with family and friends even amidst my darkest days. I've watched Northstar grow into a firm with over $1 billion in holdings. I've seen my kids become young adults and begin lives of their own.

Everyone inevitably experiences such times of adversity and advantage. While we must hurt and grieve our losses and setbacks, we must never give up building the life that we dream of having. We must push through and find the strength within to step out in faith and keep going. We must not overlook the blessings, whether small or large, that we've been given each day. We must remember to reach out to others even during our loneliest times, recognizing that we are all in this thing called life together. Gradually, I've come to see the painful seasons and occasional agonies of life as opportunities to pause momentarily and reassess my investment of resources. Those times help me clarify the legacy I want to leave. They remind me of the fleeting impermanence of this life and the importance of engaging with the present moments I'm given today.

The Bible cautions us, "Yet you do not know what your life will be like tomorrow. You are just a vapor that appears for a while and then vanishes away" (James 4:14, NASB). This verse comes to mind each winter when I'm skiing down a pristine-powdered slope in the Colorado high country or riding my horse along a mountain trail. It's so cold I can see my breath in the frosty air for a few seconds. Despite all the technological advancements that continue to increase the average life expectancy, our time here is relatively short in light of eternity. It's like a vapor, a mist, and then our time is up. Consequently, we must construct our lives—and our legacy—with intentionality and purpose each day.

FOUR QUARTERS

How do we make the most of our time? If you divide your life into quarters, recalling Bob Buford's sports metaphor in his book *Halftime*, then you begin by recognizing the different seasons and rhythms of your life. During the first quarter of your life, the focus is on developing your body and mind, experiencing the world around you with almost an immortal bliss. At this stage, most kids aren't responsible for providing the income for their families, placing a roof over their heads, and keeping food on the table. They can enjoy the wonder of learning and maturing into adulthood as they discover who they really are and the purpose they feel called to pursue.

During the second quarter, some people go on to secure a college education while others enter the workforce on a full time basis. This season emphasizes exploration of newfound adulthood, identifying and firming up your belief system, potentially falling in love and starting a family. These years can be challenging times as well, especially as you begin to grow into your responsibilities with marriage, children, career, and work-life balance.

Going into the third quarter until your mid-fifties, you build your career and nurture your family. This season marks the passage into the second half of your life, which often brings a shift from material success to spiritual realization and significance, as we discussed last chapter. During this transition, you decide what you want your final years to look like and how you want to spend the resources and capabilities you've worked so hard to earn and refine.

Ideally, your fourth quarter of life revolves around celebration and contentment. There's a natural slowing of your life's pace along with the aging process in your body. The focus is on doing what you most enjoy, spending time with beloved family members, and maintaining your health as much as you are able. These years recognize the body of work you've built and allow you to savor your accomplishments. Aware of the limited time remaining in your life, you enjoy the beauty around you and complete the legacy you will leave.

No matter which quarter you're in right now or the kind of season you're experiencing, always remember that life is short, precious, and sweet. Yes, we may have our ups and downs, but you have been given a unique gift to live on planet earth. To our human knowledge, other unique life forms like us do not exist elsewhere in the entire universe. Your one precious life is a process of ongoing discovery. We all should be grateful for life, and celebrate it to the full, as none of us know just how long we have. What we do know, however, is that our lives are finite, nothing more than a mist on the mirror of time.

SHELTER YOUR DREAMS

While we only have today, each of us continues to build a life with new stories added. We grow and change. We learn and evolve. We suffer and become even stronger.

Each of us has lessons and ideas to learn from others, even as we have our own wisdom to share with those around us as well. One of my favorite quotations, which I happened upon while I was in college, reminds us, "Success is not final, and failure is not fatal."

I keep this quote on the inside cover of my black business binder to this day, usually carrying it with me and seeing it daily. I believe in the truth these words express, reminded of the way we are all on a journey to our respective "Ithacas," and that as our journey progresses, so may our definition of Ithaca change as our life's destination. Part of your life's goal is fulfilled through the journey itself. Even if you don't arrive on the shores of your original goal, don't be afraid embrace the place where you find yourself. It may be your Ithaca in disguise and provide the setting for building a life beyond the one you've imagined.

As you build stories onto each subsequent floor of the life you're building, I urge you to make the most of their construction. Make them impactful for others, as well as for the life you're enjoying as you reach for the sky. Each of us has a finite time here on this planet, and we should try to make the most of it. Don't end up with regrets about what might have been or who you could have been if only you had made different choices. Build boldly into your future, using the finest materials available to you. Take care not to cut corners in your quality construction. Make sure you build a life structure that shelters your dreams.

Seize the moment this day, write a legacy of positive impact, and be the person that you know you can be. You are the only person on this planet in the history of time who can be the unique person you are, who can make the change and impact that only you can make. Do not squander this gift by taking it for granted, or by refusing to act upon it. If you do not do so, it may never occur, may never make the positive impact it is supposed to make. You have everything you need to build a beautiful life, one that will weather all of life's storms and endure as a legacy for generations to come.

I look forward to seeing you along the roads and seas to Ithaca, my fellow traveler. Our time is now. *Build a life to support your dreams!*

FAVORITE QUOTES, MAXIMS, AND EXPRESSIONS

Ever since I was young, I have enjoyed great quotes, maxims, and expressions. The creative use of wit, wisdom, and humor has always encouraged and impressed me, along with the power of well-chosen words. The best expressions remain timeless in their wisdom and ideas conveyed. From my collection of well over one hundred, I've curated fifty of my all-time favorites for you below. Attributions are provided based on the best of my knowledge; anonymous or well-known sayings do not have an attribution. I hope these words inspire you, motivate you, challenge you, and leave you with a smile!

1)   Pigs get fed, and hogs get slaughtered.

2)   What can take you a moment to buy, can take you a lifetime to sell.

3)   A bird in the hand, or two in the bush.

4)   You make your money on the buy.

5)   Our doubts are traitors, and makes us lose the good we oft might win by fearing to attempt.

--Shakespeare, Measure for Measure, 1.4

6)   Success is not final, and failure is not fatal.

7)   We know what we are, but know not what we may be.

--Shakespeare, Hamlet, 4.5

8)   "If you think you are beaten, you are
     If you think you dare not, you don't,
     If you like to win, but you think you can't
     It is almost certain you won't.

     If you think you'll lose, you're lost
     For out of the world we find,
     Success begins with a fellow's will
     It's all in the state of mind.

     If you think you are outclassed, you are
     You've got to think high to rise,

You've got to be sure of yourself before
You can ever win a prize.

Life's battles don't always go
To the stronger or faster man,
But soon or late the man who wins
Is the man WHO THINKS HE CAN!"

--Walter D. Wintle

9) Every champion was once a contender that refused to give up.

--Rocky Balboa

10) There are two great days in a person's life- the day we are born and the day we discover why.

--William Barclay

11) Stay away from negative people, they have a problem for every solution.

--Albert Einstein

12) The most reliable way to predict the future, is to create it.

13) I'd rather attempt to do something great and fail, than to attempt to do nothing and succeed.

--Robert H. Schuller

14) You are confined only by the walls you build yourself.

15) F.E.A.R. has two meanings: Forget Everything And Run, OR Face Everything And Rise. The choice is yours.

16) The question isn't who is going to let me; it's who is going to stop me.

--Ayn Rand

17) Don't make a permanent decision for your temporary emotion.

18) There are no secrets to success. It is the result of preparation, hard work, and learning from failure.

-- Colin Powell

19) There is only one thing that makes a dream impossible to achieve- the fear of failure.

--Paulo Coelho

20) You cannot control everything that happens to you; you can only control the way you respond to what happens. In your response is your power.

21) Just remember: the people that say "your dreams are impossible" have already quit on theirs.

--Grant Cardone

22) Success consists of going from failure to failure without loss of enthusiasm.

--Winston Churchill

23) My mission in life is not merely to survive, but to thrive; and to do so with some passion, some compassion, some humor, and some style.

--Maya Angelou

24) Talent is given, greatness is earned.

25) It's hard to soar with eagles, when you're floppin' around on the ground with turkeys.

26) The true entrepreneur is a doer, not a dreamer.

--Nolan Bushnell

27) Always make your future bigger than your past.

--Dan Sullivan

28) The greatest solution of all is to live and work in partnership with yourself, your family and friends, your work and community, your nation, your world, nature, and spirit.

--Marc Allen

29) The origin of innovation and entrepreneurship is a creative mindset.

--Michael Harris

30) Inspiring someone else to follow their dreams is the hope of anyone who has the courage to follow their own.

--Dawn Garcia

31) A man must be big enough to admit his mistakes, smart enough to profit from them, and strong enough to correct them.

--John C. Maxwell

32) Good fortune is what happens when opportunity meets with planning.

--Thomas Edison

33) You and I have a rendezvous with destiny. We will preserve for our children this, the last best hope of man on earth, or we will sentence them to take the first step into a thousand years of darkness. If we fail, at least let our children and our children's children say of us we justified our brief moment here. We did all that could be done.

--Ronald Reagan

34) We can't all be Washingtons, but we can all be patriots.

--Charles F. Browne

35) The cement of this union is the heart-blood of every American.

--Thomas Jefferson

36) America is much more than a geographical fact. It is a political and moral fact—the first community in which men set out in principle to institutionalize freedom, responsible government, and human equality.

--Adlai Stevenson

37) Where liberty dwells, there is my country.

--Benjamin Franklin

38) Freedom lies in being bold.

--Robert Frost

39) The earth will not continue to offer its harvest, except with faithful stewardship. We cannot say we love the land and then take steps to destroy it for use by future generations.

--Pope John Paul II

40) The master of the garden is the one who waters it, trims the branches, plants the seeds, and pulls the weeds. If you merely stroll through the garden, you are but an acolyte.

--Vera Nazarian

41) The thing that lies at the foundation of positive change, the way I see it, is service to a fellow human being.

--Lee Iacocca

42) At the end of life we will not be judged by how many diplomas we have received, how much money we have made, how many great things we have done. We will be judged by "I was hungry, and you gave me something to eat, I was naked and you clothed me. I was homeless, and you took me in."

--Mother Teresa

43) Everybody can be great...because anybody can serve. You don't have to have a college degree to serve. You don't have to make your subject and verb agree to serve. You only need a heart full of grace. A soul generated by love.

--Martin Luther King Jr.

44) Don't be afraid to give up the good to go for the great.

--John D. Rockefeller

45) There are two types of people who will tell you that you cannot make a difference in this world: those who are afraid to try and those who are afraid you will succeed.

--Ray Goforth

46) Successful people do what unsuccessful people are not willing to do. Don't wish it were easier; wish you were better.

--Jim Rohn

47) The ones who are crazy enough to think they can change the world, are the ones that do.

--Anonymous

48) People who succeed have momentum. The more they succeed, the more they want to succeed, and the more they find a way to succeed. Similarly, when someone is failing, the tendency is to get on a downward spiral that can even become a self-fulfilling prophecy.

--Tony Robbins

49) Don't let the fear of losing be greater than the excitement of winning.

--Robert Kiyosaki

50) Opportunities don't happen. You create them.

--Chris Grosser